TENACIOUS

TENACIOUS

How God Used a Terminal Diagnosis to Turn a Family and a Football Team into Champions

JEREMY AND JENNIFER WILLIAMS
WITH ROB SUGGS

THOMAS NELSON
Since 1798

NASHVILLE   DALLAS   MEXICO CITY   RIO DE JANEIRO

Published in Nashville, Tennessee, by Thomas Nelson. Thomas Nelson is a registered trademark of Thomas Nelson, Inc.

Published in association with the literary agency of WordServe Literary Group, Ltd., www.wordserveliterary.com.

Thomas Nelson, Inc., titles may be purchased in bulk for educational, business, fund-raising, or sales promotional use. For information, please e-mail SpecialMarkets@ ThomasNelson.com.

Unless otherwise noted, Scripture quotations are taken from the Holy Bible, New International Version®, NIV®. © 1973, 1978, 1984, 2011 by Biblica, Inc.™ Used by permission of Zondervan. All rights reserved worldwide. www.zondervan.com.

Scripture quotation marked NKJV is from THE NEW KING JAMES VERSION®. © 1982 by Thomas Nelson, Inc. Used by permission. All rights reserved.

Scripture quotation marked NLT is from *Holy Bible*, New Living Translation. © 1996, 2004, 2007. Used by permission of Tyndale House Publishers, Inc., Wheaton, Illinois 60189. All rights reserved.

Scripture quotation marked KJV is from the King James Version of the Bible.

Library of Congress Cataloging-in-Publication Data

Williams, Jeremy, 1971-

Tenacious : how God used a terminal diagnosis to turn a family and a football team into champions / Jeremy and Jennifer Williams with Rob Suggs.

pages cm.

Includes bibliographical references.

ISBN 978-1-59555-523-6 (pbk.)

1. Williams, Jeremy, 1971- 2. Football coaches--United States--Biography. 3. Football coaches--United States--Religious life. 4. Amyotrophic lateral sclerosis--Patients--Religious life. 5. Families--Religious life. I. Williams, Jennifer, 1972- II. Suggs, Rob. III. Title.

GV939.W52A3 2013

796.332092--dc23

[B]

2013004064

Printed in the United States of America

13 14 15 16 17 18 RRD 6 5 4 3 2 1

For God's glory

CONTENTS

1. MOVE THAT BUS!   1

2. COLUMBUS DAYS   19

3. BOY MEETS GIRL   33

4. FINDING FOCUS   43

5. THE LEGEND OF THE GEORGIA ASSASSIN   61

6. HIGH-IMPACT FAITH   73

7. LOVE, PERIOD   85

8. THE GOOD LIFE   97

9. STEPPING UP   111

10. STANDING FIRM   127

11. BREAKING THROUGH   135

12. CHIP'S STORY   151

13. A FRAGILE GIFT   165

14. GUT CHECK   181

CONTENTS

15. WE DO WHAT WE DO   191

16. WELCOME TO THE FRONT LINE   203

17. A SEASON FOR MIRACLES   215

18. THREE WISE MEN   229

19. EXTREME HOME MIRACLES   239

20. IN HIS GRIP   255

ACKNOWLEDGMENTS   267

NOTES   271

ABOUT THE AUTHORS   273

1

MOVE THAT BUS!

THE PLAYGROUND TEEMED WITH CHILDREN: LAUGHING, shouting, expending enough natural energy to power a small town.

Not far away, a group of mothers huddled together and kept watch: chatting, laughing, tending to the occasional skinned knee.

They were also tending a quiet conspiracy. Jennifer Williams simply hadn't caught on yet.

"You know what you need, girl?" Christina asked her that January morning in 2009. "You need an extreme home makeover."

"Tell me about it," Jennifer replied with a smirk.

"I'm serious. You know, the TV show—where they come out and knock down your house and put up a new one. Wouldn't that be awesome?"

"Oh yeah!" Jennifer laughed. "Nice to dream, but I've got to make do with what I've got."

"Oh, don't get me wrong," said Christina quickly. "I love your house. It's adorable. But it's not really set up for, well, *accessibility*— not for Jacob. And soon it's not going to work for Jeremy."

She offered this last part tentatively, knowing she was treading on rough terrain.

"It's true." Jennifer sighed. "Jacob can't reach anything he needs from his wheelchair. It's all up too high. He can't even reach his toothbrush by himself. There's no room for him to wheel through the kitchen, and he can't go anywhere outside by himself because he can't get across the grass and the gravel drive."

"I can't even imagine how tough all that is."

"Well, Jacob's used to it. It's all he's ever known. But it breaks my heart, Christina. Jeremy's too. Right now he can help Jacob, but in six months, a year . . ."

Christina reached out and squeezed her friend's hand. With her nursing background, she understood about caring for medical needs, and she knew life would only become tougher for Jennifer. That family needed a miracle.

Jennifer Williams's five-year-old son, Jacob, had been born with spina bifida, meaning he had spinal problems. He couldn't move his legs. And the previous year Jennifer's football-coach husband had been diagnosed with Lou Gehrig's disease, a progressive and incurable affliction of the nerve cells. At the very most, Jeremy Williams had just a few years to live. And during that time, little by little, his body would lose motor control.

The Williamses lived in a little country home in Pine Mountain Valley, an unincorporated but close-knit community in Harris County, Georgia. The house had been their dream home until recently, when their life had taken a couple of left turns.

Jennifer often shared her challenges with this little group of mothers, who gathered regularly to let their children play together. She saw them as a powerful support group that had materialized not a moment too soon in her life. Her two guys had special needs. But she also had a need—for emotional and spiritual encouragement. Her friends loved her, and there were days when they provided the little touch of grace that kept her from despair.

"Well, I still think you ought to apply for the home make-over thing," Christina said. "Who could possibly deserve it more, Jen? Just fill out the application. Why not?" Christina thrust a printout into her hands.

Jennifer couldn't believe her friend had gone to the trouble of getting an application. "Thanks," she said. "I'll think about it." But she knew she'd throw the thing away as soon as she got home.

A couple of months passed before Naomi, another friend from the play group, approached Jennifer. "Hi! I've got something for you." And she handed her another application for *Extreme Makeover: Home Edition*.

"This again?" laughed Jennifer. "Did Christina put you up to this?"

Naomi produced an innocent expression while Adrianne added, "It's a great idea, Jennifer. You guys deserve it!"

"Just fill it out," Naomi pressed. "Go for it."

"I don't know, Naomi. You know how much I love the home we have. Let me think about it."

But she'd thought about it already, and she just couldn't wrap her mind around the idea of being on a television show. She could imagine God miraculously healing her men much more easily than Hollywood swooping in to make her home more accessible. It seemed like hitting the lottery or suddenly inheriting a million dollars from an unknown relative. Fantasy stuff.

When Melissa Acton brought her a third application, Jennifer sniffed out the conspiracy. "You're all together in this, aren't you?"

"Guilty," said Melissa. "Your sisters have been plotting behind your back. We love you, and we want you to have a brand-new home. Now are you going to cooperate and fill out that form, or are we going to have to fill it out ourselves?"

"Melissa, you girls can fill out forms to your hearts' content. God gave us our house, and I'm going to try and make it work."

It was a battle of feminine wills. Every five weeks, one of the women showed up with another application, but Jennifer held the line. Then, in October 2009, the local newspaper carried an article announcing that ABC-TV's *Extreme Makeover: Home Edition* was looking for a Georgia family to accept one of their remarkable home constructions.

Now her friends were insistent. Naomi said, "Jennifer, your chances are fifty times better now! You just have to compete with people from your own state."

That same day, another friend—one from *outside* the play group—called Jennifer. Ava Medders was the wife of Jeremy's best friend, Chip. She, too, had read the article, and she challenged Jennifer to pray about such an extraordinary opportunity.

"Jennifer, have you considered that this might not only be about the house? This could be God's way of spreading your story across the nation. You need to pray about it."

Jennifer had to admit that she hadn't done that. Maybe it was time. So on the way home from the feed store that day, after buying supplies for her horses, she finally raised the subject with God. *Lord, you know my girlfriends have been after me about this house thing,* she prayed, eyes open, as she drove. *I just don't know if it's your plan, so you're going to have to make it clear to me.*

Then she did something a bit spiritually daring. She made God a proposition. *If somebody new gets involved in this—someone who hasn't said a word up to now—well, I'm going to believe you want me to do this, and I'm going to apply to that show.*

Asking God for a sign was uncommon for Jennifer. She knew Bible heroes like Gideon had done it, but she rarely had.

It felt like a crazy thing to do. But somehow it also felt right. She drove the rest of the way home with a sense of peace.

It was just about then that another Jennifer, a play-group friend named Jennifer Vaughn, decided that God wasn't going to leave her alone. She was aware of the campaign to get the Williamses to apply for *Extreme Makeover: Home Edition* but she had refrained from joining in. If Jennifer Williams didn't want to apply, she'd figured, then that was that; she wasn't going to get involved. But something kept nagging at her.

Okay, God, she finally prayed, *I'll do something.* And since she happened to be sitting in front of her computer at the moment, she decided to put out a message to her Facebook friends. She would tell them about Jeremy and Jennifer Williams and how they needed ABC-TV to build them a new house. She would ask them to write letters to ABC recommending the Williamses for their show.

That's when the letter-writing campaign began.

EASY AS ABC

By the time Jennifer Williams found out about the other Jennifer's involvement, the December 1 entry deadline was just about to pass.

Jennifer V, who had followed up her Facebook messages by working with the other play-group moms, called Jennifer W's mother for pictures to enclose with an application. Mom couldn't resist telling her daughter. And when she did, Jennifer W suddenly realized what it all meant. A previously uninvolved friend had gotten involved—her prayer condition. She ran to tell Jeremy.

"God gave you confirmation, babe," he said, "I guess you have to go ahead and let them make you a TV star now!"

Jeremy texted a message to Ava Medders, who had volunteered earlier to help make the application video. Jeremy's text contained the familiar words that always preceded the "reveal" on *Extreme Makeover: Home Edition*: "Move that bus!"

Ava quickly texted a reply: "I'm going to remind you that you said that!"

Jeremy and Jennifer laughed over that one. They finally completed an application, and Ava posted it just in time, fedexing it to arrive right on the December 1 deadline. But on November 30, while the application was still en route, Jennifer's phone rang. "This is the ABC television network calling," said a voice on the other end. "Am I speaking to Mrs. Williams?"

"This is she," Jennifer admitted, mystified. She knew the application was still en route. Why was ABC calling her now? After about twenty minutes of interview questions, she finally managed, "Excuse me. But can I ask how y'all know about us?"

"Well, we've received a few letters from your friends." The woman began thumbing through them, identifying the writers. "I have a letter here from a Brian and Melissa Acton. There is also a letter from someone named Charlie Williams."

"Charlie wrote you?"

Charlie Williams (no relation) had gone to high school with Jeremy and had attended church with Jennifer in Columbus, Georgia. How had *he* gotten into the middle of this thing?

The woman said, "This letter from Charlie Williams—it's one of the most touching letters about a family I've ever read. So we were following up to get more information about your family."

"We *did* send an application," said Jennifer. "You should have it tomorrow."

"You did?" The woman became very excited. "Oh, that's *wonderful!*"

It quickly became clear that more than a few letters were involved. Nearly all Jennifer's friends had written the show— Jeremy's too. A cousin named Amber Richter had contacted a number of folks from nearby Meriwether County, where Jeremy coached the Greenville High football team. She'd introduced herself and asked people to put in a word for the Williamses. Carol Lane, the superintendent of the county school system, received an e-mail from Lee Riley, a close friend of Jeremy's. Soon pretty much all of Meriwether County was writing letters.

To this day, no one can account for the thousand or more letters ABC received. Jeremy and Jennifer can only assume that when God really wants something to happen, he's more stubborn even than she is. Or maybe a better word is *tenacious.* He holds fast to his perfect plan.

Still, several other families were in the running, and the show's executives had to make a final decision. Jeremy and Jennifer waited nervously for the Sunday morning when they and the other families would receive either a door knock or a phone call. The phone call meant gentle condolences. The door knock meant that the *Extreme Makeover* bus was sitting outside.

And if that happened, then miracles really were possible and dreams really could come true, even in the quiet Georgia countryside.

COME OUT, COME OUT,
WHEREVER YOU ARE

On the big morning, a bus moved through the quiet highways of Harris County. Aboard was Ty Pennington, the Georgia native who hosted the TV show. With him were three of the show's regular designers plus some special guest members of the team— Michael Oher of the Baltimore Ravens, Leigh Anne Tuohy, and Sean Tuohy. These were the people who had inspired the book and movie, *The Blind Side*.

While traveling they filmed segments introducing the Williams family. Soon the bus and the production trucks were pulling up outside Jennifer and Jeremy's thirties-era farmhouse. It sat quiet in the solemn calm of a country morning. Not a Williams was in sight.

Ty and his friends approached the front yard, and he pulled out his megaphone. "Gooooood morning, Williams family!" he shouted. He called out each of their names and invited them to come out and celebrate the good news.

And the house continued to sit on its hill, unimpressed.

"Jeremy! Jennifer! Josie! Jacob! Come on out!" he shouted again. They couldn't *possibly* have decided to be somewhere else, could they? The team members looked at each other and shrugged.

Finally there came the sound of scraping wood. The red-painted door pushed open and the Williamses came spilling out, with Jennifer's delirious shrieks shattering the quiet. She emerged with Jacob on her shoulder and an excited Josie skipping behind. Jeremy appeared last of all, helped along by a crutch and his trademark grin. The cameras took it all in.

Once they were off the air, Ty asked, "What in the world took you guys so long?"

Jennifer explained that one of the house's unique features was a front door that opened very begrudgingly. Once it was locked, you had to really want to get the door open again. Then you had to turn the bolt as you pushed your knee forcefully into the frame. The Williamses really wanted to get outside to greet their visitors; they just needed to convince the door to cooperate. All the more reason a new house was a good idea.

The comical delay would be edited out of the telecast, though it did give everyone a big laugh on the beautiful Sunday. However, comedy wasn't the order of the day; this show would focus on deeper emotions. No one who experienced it, either in person or as a viewer, would ever forget it.

Since its first episodes in 2003, *Extreme Makeover: Home Edition* had become known as a reality show with a difference. It was the brainchild of the creators of *Fear Factor*, *Big Brother*, and the original *Extreme Makeover*, which focused more on personal style. But while those shows often catered to thrills or vanity or pettiness—staples of reality TV—this series aimed for the better angles of the viewers' nature. It sought out people who genuinely needed and deserved help, whether in a family or a community. The show's heartwarming solutions made for satisfying television.

The team accomplished each episode's miracles in a fast week of construction—with donated materials and volunteer labor. During that week, the audience would follow the fortunate family on a special vacation provided by the show. Then the family would return for the reveal. The bus would move, and a beautiful new structure would stand waiting for them.

But that was all still in the future that first morning, as the Williams family mingled with the *EM* team. Big Michael Oher of the Baltimore Ravens—six-foot-four and 315 pounds—scooped up little Jacob as if he were a football. Jeremy and Jennifer chatted with everyone. Ty Pennington then announced that the Williamses would be flown to Crested Butte, Colorado, to the Adaptive Sports Center, a wonderful facility that helps people with special needs enjoy skiing, tubing, and other vigorous activities.

Jennifer screamed once again. Somewhere, the play-group ladies were chuckling.

ROCKY MOUNTAIN HIGH

The vacation at Crested Butte had a dreamlike quality to it. An epic snowstorm had painted the world white and fluffy the day before they arrived. This alone was almost surreal for anyone born and bred in the South. The Adaptive Sports Center staff handled the four visitors like royalty throughout the week, as did the trio of ABC-TV people who followed them around: a nice lady who coordinated things, a cameraman, and a sound technician.

On their first morning, Jeremy and Jacob started with sit-down skis. A friendly guide named Danielle, tied to Jeremy's ski sled, regulated his speed. Meanwhile the two girls skied on the beginner slopes. At one point, Jennifer turned her head just in time to see a large object streak by at high velocity. It was Jacob, shouting and having the time of his life. For this one week, it was as if he had awakened to a different reality—one in which he could do all the things that other boys did and be defined by the adventures he chose rather than the limitations that had chosen him.

Jacob had been very nervous about these activities, as any

six-year-old might be. But at breakfast, one of the ski instructors, Lisa, had made friends with him. Making friends is perhaps the greatest of Jacob's talents; to meet him is to bond with him almost instantly. After a few minutes of eating and laughing together, Lisa said, "Let's go hit it, Jacob!"

He held up his hands and shouted, "Let's go!" And in no time he was flying past his startled mother. Not long after that, he was leaning one way or the other with expert precision, directing the sled. It was the most amazing day of his life.

It wasn't long before Jeremy, too, was skiing down every slope on the mountain. He was tubing, skiing, shouting, and laughing. He hadn't grown up on snowy slopes, but he found himself reveling in the winter sports. He squeezed all the joy out of these few days that he could, knowing he was unlikely to ever be able to do these things again.

At one point during that idyllic vacation, the ABC-TV people brought a monitor to show what was happening back home. Ty and the gang had come up with a brainstorm. Who better to bring down a football coach's house than a football team? In full equipment, Jeremy's Greenville Patriots came after the Williamses' old house as if it were a rival quarterback. They knocked down walls and destroyed property with relish as ABC and ESPN announcers called the action.

Jennifer thought, *Look at all that dust! Thank you, Lord, for providing for us!*

Jeremy's feelings were a little more mixed. "They're killing our house!" he said. There was something painful in watching one's dream house demolished, even knowing something better would replace it. Jeremy thought about his old life, the person he had been before he had come to know Jesus Christ. Putting the old self to death in order to become a new creation in Christ had been uncomfortable too. Before every resurrection, there had to be a cross.

The four of them whispered silent good-byes to their old premises two thousand miles away and realized that yes, their future was going to be very different.

A SURPRISE VISITOR

On the third day of their vacation, the Williamses were resting at the foot of the slopes, near a fire pit, enjoying cups of hot chocolate and deciding what they wanted to do next. A cell phone was brought, and it was time to hear from Ty again. Josie and Jacob wondered if they'd get to open the special package now. Back at home, the host had presented them with a beautifully wrapped box and told them not to open it until he said it was okay.

Sure enough, Ty let them open the box. It held a carrot. The first thing Jennifer thought of was a horse, since she had a passion for them. But Ty instructed them to look for someone who might need it. And there, building a snowman that needed a carrot nose, stood young TV star Demi Lovato. The producers had discovered that both kids were big fans of Demi, particularly her Disney Channel movie, *Camp Rock*.

Jacob didn't recognize her at first. Her hair was darker than he had seen it on TV. But Josie figured it all out quickly, and she and her heroine walked off, hand in hand. They were all being herded to an indoor venue, around a cozy fireplace, where Demi's band was set up for a musical performance.

Jacob was still confused though. "Don't you know who that is?" Jennifer asked as she wheeled Jacob through the hotel. "From *Camp Rock*?"

"But is that really her?" Jacob was skeptical. This whole Colorado place was amazing enough, but now Disney Channel characters were showing up.

Jennifer assured her son it was really Demi Lovato, and he took off in his chair, happily starstruck.

As the room was being prepared for filming, Demi asked the kids to sing their favorite *Camp Rock* song. They began, and she joined in, her band playing along. Then, after everyone laughed and clapped, Demi said, "I want to sing one just for you, Jeremy and Jennifer—not for the cameras." And she began to sing a song about falling in love and finding out that person was even better than you'd imagined. Jeremy and Jennifer felt as if the song told the story of their relationship, and both began to cry.

Then, as the cameras rolled, Demi sang about ripples—about how they begin as tiny rings and move out across the water to become great waves that change destinies. Jeremy and Jennifer, holding hands, were thoughtful as they listened to this one. They thought about their story and their desire that someone, somewhere, could be blessed or given courage from it.

Maybe their story could ripple across Georgia, across the nation, and even beyond it. They wanted no glory or fame for themselves, just the satisfaction of knowing their struggles were part of a greater, more redemptive picture that God was painting.

A Cloud of Witnesses

By Thursday, the family was back on a plane, climbing into the clouds and then descending to the busy Atlanta airport. In ordinary circumstances, dream-vacation getaways give way to humdrum familiarity. We all have to come down from the mountaintop sometime. But not yet—not for the Williams family. They were returning to a brand-new home, one they could not even visualize. They only knew it would be beyond their greatest hopes for a new house. ABC-TV would see to that. Crested Butte had been wonderful, but the best was yet to come.

Josie and Jacob had a thousand questions: "What will it look like?" "Will I have a bigger room?" "What if they lose my toys?" Jeremy and Jennifer could only smile, shrug, and assure their kids that there was no way they would be disappointed.

A limousine delivered the family to a hotel in the town of LaGrange, just twenty-five miles north of home. They discovered that they'd been brought back a little early for an added surprise. On Friday, they were taken to nearby Greenville, where Jeremy had coached high school football for years. As Jeremy and Jennifer stepped from the limousine at Greenville High, a crowd of familiar faces bustled around them: family, friends, high-school football players, college friends, and Memphis State football teammates—even Hines Ward, the Super Bowl MVP and *Dancing with the Stars* champion.

The reunion was overwhelming, and what lay before them brought them to tears: a brand-new field house for the team. The old, hardscrabble weights and lockers had given way to a beautiful, state-of-the-art facility with all-new equipment, a washer and dryer for the jerseys, and a huge television set with high-tech software editing programs for game breakdowns. The players' old uniforms were now replaced by beautiful new jerseys and pants and helmets. An extra locker with Jacob's name on it was marked *Mayor*. Jacob was issued a key to it and told that every time he showed up before a game, he could use his locker.

All this, of course, was a gift of grace. The Williamses had no idea that the generosity of the sponsors would extend to the high school and the student-athletes. Jeremy remembered his arrival at the school only eight years ago. There had been almost no facilities at all. The coaches had brought in the weights themselves.

The new field house would be named for Jeremy, but he saw it as an altar of praise to the God who makes all things new, who blesses whole communities and not just individuals. He whispered a prayer of thanks for the kindness of both friends and strangers, through whom God had blessed the school and the program that was his heart and soul. He knew the time was approaching when he could no longer coach these young men. But long after his strength had finally failed, the doors of this room would remain open. New generations of young men would be reminded of the powers of faith and goodness.

And this surprise was only a preview to the main event of the next day. The limousine had one more stop to make.

Saturday morning, Jeremy and Jennifer looked at each other and smiled as the limo made its way south toward Pine Mountain Valley. Once it arrived at their house, there was a twenty-minute wait until the producers were ready to film. The windows of the vehicle were darkened so the Williamses could not see out. They could hear a crowd of people and feel the tingle of excitement in the air. And even without being able to see, Jennifer knew exactly where the car was. "They've paved our gravel driveway!" she said. "Jacob, you're going to be able to play outside now!"

The car indeed came to a stop; they were home. There would be surprises far more thrilling than pavement, but for Jennifer, this alone was a wondrous thing—something that would change her son's life.

Jeremy and Jennifer joined hands with their children and prayed that all their actions, all their words, would honor Christ.

As Jeremy listened to the muffled sounds of a crowd outside, it was possible to think of another day like this one, a future day. That occasion, that homecoming day, would shine even brighter. Paul the apostle once compared life on earth to seeing through a dim glass, much like the darkened windows of the limo. Yet someday, he wrote, we will step beyond that glass, and we will see God face-to-face (see 1 Cor. 13:12).

There is another verse about the "cloud of witnesses" that surrounds us, cheering us on as we run the race that is this life (Heb. 12:1). Someday, the Bible promises, we will walk into a new world, reunited with our encouragers. A new and glistening home, far beyond our imagining, awaits us, just as it awaited Jeremy and his family that morning. Then, as now, God delights in making his children happy.

As they waited, Jeremy thought back over the winding, ever-surprising road that had brought them to this moment. He remembered his youth and the remarkable circumstances that had brought Jennifer to him. He also recalled an unforgettable fork in the road, when he could have chosen the darker path. Yet Christ had taken hold of him and changed him forever.

Jeremy thought about his years of college football, and he remembered coming home to create a new life as a coach, a husband, and then a father. He recalled the moments of grief, the crises that had arisen to threaten his family's future. There had been pain as well as joy. But he could still say from the depths of his heart that God is good.

Jeremy and Jennifer savored the joy of the moment until the signal came to open the car doors. "Welcome home, Williams family!" shouted Ty Pennington, though he was drowned out by the roars of the gathered crowd. As the limo door opened, it seemed as if the deafening exultation of the throng broke right into the interior and pulled Jeremy out. He grinned and waved as he stood next to the big bus that blocked the family's view of the house.

"Thank y'all for coming!" Jennifer called out, coming right behind him.

The Williamses were given a couple of seconds to greet their friends, their cloud of witnesses, at the fence. Jennifer quickly picked out the faces of her parents, her brother, and her sister-in-law.

The family wanted to greet everyone, but the scene was chaotic and the cameras were rolling. Only later would they realize just how many people were gathered there. An overhead camera would pan the crowd and show a vast throng of well-wishers. They came from the community, from friends, from family, from sports, from all the people who loved and admired Jeremy and Jennifer Williams.

The crowd managed to fall a little quieter as Ty said to the family, "What's behind this bus is going to make your lives a little easier."

Then he knelt beside Jacob and asked if he wanted to deliver those three powerful words. Of course he did, but everyone had been waiting for that moment. The crowd was loud enough to be heard in the next county.

"Move that bus!"

2

COLUMBUS DAYS

HOMETOWNS MAY NOT DEFINE US FOREVER, BUT THEY leave their mark. Time passes; other locales help to sculpt us. But that first community, the setting of our childhood, is the place where our true selves take root. Whoever we may become, we will always be that native son—or daughter—of one specific place and time that is not quite like any other.

For Jeremy and Jennifer Williams, the place was Columbus, Georgia. The time was the early eighties. From there, the story would take many twists and turns. But every road leads back here.

Columbus, Georgia, sits on the Alabama border, where the Chattahoochee River ambles by on its way to the Florida line. The people here wonder, why hurry? This is a good place to linger.

A magazine recently named Columbus America's fourth most livable city, and the reasons are many. It's a city that feels like a town—quiet and orderly, bustling but not crowded. Fort Benning, home of the US Infantry, houses more than 120,000 soldiers, family members, retirees, civilians, and contractors just to the south. Columbus cares most about family, church, and country. It's vintage middle-class America.

Across a bridge, on the Alabama side of the river, stands Columbus's eager little brother, Phenix City. Its proud residents would have you know that *Business Week* identifies it as the most affordable suburb in America for raising a family. Yet Little Brother has also been somewhat of a prodigal son. In the 1950s yet another periodical, *Look*, called Phenix City "the wickedest city in America."

The misadventures of that era have been well documented. A Southern-fried crime syndicate sponsored dens of every vice imaginable, preying on soldiers from Fort Benning, ballplayers from nearby Auburn University, and other wayward citizens. Hollywood's *The Phenix City Story* splashed all this dirty laundry across the silver screen.

But the good citizens cleaned up the mess. This is the part of the country where every town fancies itself the "buckle on the Bible Belt." Today Columbus and Phenix City major in home and hearth. *Family* holds high value, but that word means more than blood relations. It also encompasses community pride and mutual support. Parents raise their children to say "yes, sir" and "yes, ma'am." Aunts, uncles, cousins, and grannies are held close. Neighbors attend church together, hunt and fish together, and eventually share their retirement with a deep commitment to community that isn't much seen in the sprawling Southern metropolises of Atlanta, Charlotte, or Nashville.

There's plenty of love to go around, but not of the soft and squishy variety—not in metro Columbus. The military presence of Benning, the once-licentious streets of Phenix, and particularly the heritage of a rural and blue-collar South make for a community with a very muscular, street-tough idea of affection.

Take Robert Williams, for example. During the eighties, the years when he came of age, he loved his little brother enough to harass him on an ongoing basis. Robert was the eldest of three siblings, the trailblazer. He knew what awaited his little brother and sister on the streets and in the schools. Boys in particular needed basic survival skills, especially if they were on the scrawny side, as his brother Jeremy was.

The Williams brothers were three years apart. They shared a bedroom with their sister, Kimberly, in the cozy block house on Hunter Road until Kimberly reached an age when she needed more privacy. Then the parents gave up their own bedroom and slept on a sofa bed in the living room.

The guys were scrappy and competitive in the usual big brother/little brother dynamic. Jeremy idolized Robert and tagged along with the older guys. Given that he was running behind in age and in size, he received his share of teasing and roughhousing. But he took it all in stride, even gave back as good as he got.

Robert, for his part, was filling out like a linebacker—the position he would play in high school football. Yet the minnow had no fear of the whale. At any time, Jeremy would tackle his older brother or any of his brother's friends and begin another wrestling match. One of these bouts resulted in a broken collarbone for Jeremy, who missed a championship baseball game as a result.

KID STUFF

This neighborhood was a bustling settlement of young families. There were dozens of kids within a few blocks, and most of them seemed to be boys. All of them played baseball and football and any other game they could devise.

The Williams residence was the first house built, the one with the largest backyard, which was bounded by forest behind it and apartments beside it.

Today it sits empty and rather forlorn. As far as anyone remembers it, no one has moved in since the Williamses vacated it. But thirty years ago it was the center of civilization for any number of boys. You rose on a Saturday, donned your shorts and tee shirt, and proceeded to the Williamses' to see what was on the daily agenda.

The place had a number of adventure-ready features. In the backyard, you could rough out a reasonable baseball diamond and hit the ball with little threat to anyone's windowpanes. The apartment lot next door was a great place for bike riding. The woods lent themselves to exploring, shooting, and building forts, and you had to cut through them to get to the elementary school.

On a given week, daredevil bike stunts might be the thing. In the apartment parking lot, guys would set up makeshift ramps and jump them with their bicycles. It was all the rage until the day they showed up and found nails protruding from the ramps. The apartment manager wasn't going to abide any broken bones or lawsuits on his watch. Undaunted, the kids just found something else to do. Sledding, for instance.

The usual practice of sliding down snowy hillsides wasn't going to work in Columbus. For one thing, snow is exceedingly rare in these parts. For another, Columbus is a "fall line" city, set where the last foothills of the Appalachians meet the plains of southern Georgia; there just aren't many big hills. So the guys had to be creative about their sledding. They flattened some oversized cardboard cartons, carried them all the way to

Kendrick High—nearly two miles away—and whisked down its impressive grass slopes.

Jeremy and his best buddies, Larry Margarum and Jeff Cook, were always together, along with a rotating cast of others. They spent many nights in each other's homes, to the point that any dad had "whoopin' rights" over any Friday night guest. The fathers were mostly tough role models. Larry's dad, who was ex-military, would grab Jeremy with one fist and Jeff with another and hold them against the wall of the family room. "So you think you're tough?" he would bark in challenge. They'd laugh—nervously. Toughness was up there with faith, hope, and love as a cardinal virtue.

There was a place in that neighborhood for every boy, as long as he liked playing ball. One of the regulars was Kevin Stanley, whose family lived in the house next door to the Williamses for twenty years. He and his sister, Denise, were always up for a sandlot game. Kevin and others would show up at the Williams house to catch a ride to the East Columbus Boys Club to play league ball. Jeremy's dad would ride through the neighborhood gathering various boys and dropping them at gridirons or diamonds. It didn't matter if these kids weren't on your league team. The neighborhood itself was the only team that ultimately counted.

Hunting was not a hobby, but an obsession. It was and is the passion of virtually every male in middle Georgia. Younger boys were as likely to have pellet guns as bicycles, and the backyard woods offered a natural habitat for stalking the wild squirrel or blue jay. Even football often came in second in popularity because it conflicted with deer season. League basketball was a big loser, with quail and doves beckoning.

The Williams boys, avid hunters, had to play their basketball on Sundays. That was the day their maternal grandmother cooked for everyone. The boys had uncles who were only a little older than themselves, thus more like big brothers. They'd all get out under the basket and play five on five—Jeremy, Robert, their dad, the uncles, and assorted neighbors and friends. Girls could play if they wanted. So could younger children, as soon as they felt ready. But no mercy was given. Rebounds were bitterly contested. Elbows were jammed into rib cages. Noses were bloodied. Then everyone sat down for the blessing, ate chicken, and laughed and shared stories.

Whenever they played together, it was obvious that Robert was a tough and talented athlete, but his younger brother was relentless. Though size and strength were not on Jeremy's side, he compensated with sheer passion and focus and hustle.

Yet the closest he got to a real fight were the many occasions when he broke them up. For someone so driven, he was remarkably self-controlled—a natural team leader even when he was the youngest on the squad, which he often was. At the entry points to junior high, then high school, then college ball, he inevitably found himself the youngest and smallest player on the field. Yet his teammates listened when he spoke.

All this, and he got As and Bs at school.

This Jeremy Williams kid—he was one to watch. And by eighth grade, one set of eyes in particular was doing just that.

Junior High Confidential

There he was again—the boy in the baseball jacket!

This made three classes: gym, social studies, and her favorite class of all, science. Jennifer Bolles, eighth grader, officially had a *thing* for Jeremy Williams.

It was the classic schoolgirl crush. Jennifer kept a journal, and once she found out his name, it was splashed across many a page. *Jeremy + Jennifer.* She was certain she had found the man God had reserved just for her.

It was great to be in eighth grade and in love. The only way it could be better would be if Jeremy Williams figured out that she existed.

Day after day went by, and there was no eye contact between them. There was no conversation. She might look up and find him behind her at the water fountain. Other times he would brush by her on the way to his seat. *Say something, Jennifer! Let him know you're alive.* It wasn't happening.

Once she was sitting on the bleachers during gym class, and some girl sat next to her. Then Jeremy sat down on the girl's other side. After a few moments, the girl got up and left, and it was just Jeremy and Jennifer. But she still couldn't say anything. It was as if God was throwing her fastballs, setting her up good, and she couldn't get the bat off her shoulder. Her tongue froze every time; the words were locked within her soul. Every encounter turned Jennifer's resolve into gelatin. After a while, she resigned herself to loving her man forever, adoring him right to the grave, without actually ever meeting him.

Every day Jennifer would hurry onto the school bus so she could get a window seat on the right side. There she could press her nose up against the glass, scan the lines of backpack-laden students who were walking home, and pick out the dark-haired boy in the baseball jacket. He always wore that jacket and walked with a group of kids from his neighborhood. She knew he must live nearby.

At one point, word got out that Jeremy had mono. For several weeks his desk was empty, and it didn't matter where she sat on the bus. The boy in the jacket was off the map. If only she had the courage to send him a get-well card—or just find out when he would be better.

Then he not only returned, but a miracle occurred. He spoke to her. She regarded that as one of the most dramatic moments in her thirteen years of life.

"Can I borrow your Wite-Out?" The words just came out of the blue as they sat at their desks. Jennifer attempted to smile casually and avoid squeezing the little jar of correction fluid to a white, pasty pulp as she handed it to him.

"Thanks," he said as if it was just some ordinary moment.

Then he brushed a dash of white fluid onto his paper and handed the container back without looking up.

Jennifer said, "Do you know who I am, Jeremy? It's me, Jennifer Bolles, and I'm in love with you. I've written your name and a bunch of hearts on every possession I have for this entire school year."

As if. No, she didn't say that. She didn't say anything, just took the Wite-Out, cupped it in her hands, and thought, *He touched this. He corrected with it. I'll save it for the rest of my life.*

Jennifer took the container home and tucked it away, a precious souvenir of their first human interaction. She saved the Wite-Out for years and suspects it's still packed away somewhere.

Jeremy has no recollection of any of this.

A GIFT FROM GOD

Like any parent, Ann Williams loved her three children the same. Only *different.*

She loved them all equally and wholeheartedly. But every

child is unique; each has his or her own story. Ann regarded Jeremy, her middle child, as a direct gift from God. His birth seemed a miracle to her.

Robert was her firstborn. Then, when it was time for a second child, there was a miscarriage. It happened at the beginning of the third trimester, leaving Ann with a deep fear that Robert would never have any siblings. But almost immediately, against normal medical advice, she became pregnant again. Jeremy Williams was born on October 7, 1971. Ann thanked God and trusted that he must have a special purpose for such a child.

Perhaps it was losing a baby that made Ann Williams a bit of a worrier—not just about Jeremy, but about her whole brood. And the way her sons went after things was enough to make any sensible mom worry. They were always falling out of trees, getting thrown from bicycles, or sprinting home just ahead of hundreds of hornets. There were coyotes in the woods, poisonous snakes in the creek, huge older kids capable of breaking the leg of one of her kids. And don't even get her started on the hunting rifles.

Sometimes Ann found herself wishing they would sit quietly with a book or watch a little television. But she knew they were healthy, normal, outdoors-loving children, and she was thankful for them. There was no way she was going to keep them indoors. So she tried to be sensible and choose her battles wisely. And one of the places she drew the line at first was football. Her sons were not going to break every bone in their bodies playing that crazy game.

Robert and Jeremy protested. John, her husband, did too. He loved football, particularly college ball. He had always been a big fan of Alabama, the Crimson Tide. He could see his boys' ability, and he was eager to see what they could do in pads on a field.

He might have been more insistent but for two factors. First, he was a gentle and loving husband who wasn't prone to making demands, especially when he understood the extent to which his wife worried about physical injuries for her sons. Second, there was the church issue.

Ann had been raised a Seventh-day Adventist. The denomination emphasizes a belief that Saturday—as opposed to Sunday—is the true Sabbath, and it must be kept holy. Friday is a day of preparation, involving cooking, extra cleaning, prayer, and readiness. Then Friday sunset to Saturday sunset is a day of full observance. This means no work—home or business. For most Adventists, Saturday also means no purely secular recreation. Quite often, league sports are specifically mentioned in this context. Television, apart from shows with Christian content, is to be avoided.

When the kids were younger, Ann took them to church every Saturday. As she drove along, they'd watch sadly through the windows as other boys and girls were out playing, some of them dressed in impressive football or baseball uniforms. Ann felt their pain; it was very difficult for her not to give in and make them happy. Yet the pastors were very firm in their teaching on this matter. It was a matter of obedience to God's commandments, a test of spiritual integrity. "Train up a child in the way he should go," they urged, quoting the book of Proverbs, "and when he is old, he will not depart from it" (Prov. 22:6 KJV).

True, she thought, *but* . . .

She would stand with her husband at the window, listening to the shouts, watching the joys of their kids playing their games. Robert was good at every game he played. Jeremy was a natural. When they were involved in sports, they were truly in their element.

Could it be that this, too—this athleticism—was a gift from God?

Would the Lord truly be deeply offended just because they pursued it on a particular day of the week?

A GIFT FROM MOTHER

Little by little, over time, Ann found herself rethinking the issue. All her kids wanted was to play sports, which included playing on Saturdays—even Kimberly was into softball. Robert, being the oldest, had to weather the strictest decisions. When Jeremy began raising the same question, Ann had been worn down considerably. By the time he was eight or nine, Ann knew something had to give.

She talked to her pastors, and they said what they always did: "Don't be worldly. Be obedient to God." But to Ann it wasn't that simple.

For one thing, these were her husband's kids too. He believed in God, but he was not an Adventist. This idea of taking Saturdays away made no sense to him, though he had been loving and accepting of her beliefs. Wasn't it Ann's Christian duty to be sensitive to *his* wishes? And didn't he have the same rights to put his boys on a team as she did to put them in a pew?

More important, in the long run her children would have to make their own decisions about following Christ. What decisions were they likely to make if they only saw the church as something that took away the things they loved?

"I don't believe God will hold this against me," she finally told her husband. "He knows I have to be a mother and I have to be a wife. He is love, not just a lot of *thou shalt nots*. We've raised our kids in a Christian home. We've taught them about God. No, I don't believe he will hold this against me. Do you, John?"

Of course he didn't. And when it came time for Robert and Jeremy to sign up for Little League baseball, Ann finally said yes. Jeremy whooped and cheered and hugged her neck—Dad's too. "But don't forget your part of the deal," said Ann. "On Saturday mornings, you will be in church. You'll participate every week, and you'll go to Vacation Bible School during the summer. Then, after church, we'll drive you to the field."

Jeremy excelled at baseball from the beginning. He could play nearly any position, could run and field and hit and throw, and his first season was a big success. Then baseball was over and it was summertime—time for going to the pool, hanging out at Lake Walter Richards, riding bikes, and just being kids.

When fall rolled around, John started talking about football again. Ann still wasn't ready for that. But by that time the organized-sports genie was out of the bottle. If he couldn't play football, suggested other parents—why not soccer? So Jeremy played that game, and again he starred. It was a game for hustling, and Jeremy was all about hustle.

The big surprise was just how physical that "nonphysical" sport could be. "Did you see 'em taking kicks to the chin? Getting tangled up with each other?" asked John. "If he can play this game, why can't he play football? Do you really think Jeremy isn't tough enough for that game?"

"Yeah!" said Jeremy. "Why not, Mom? I won't get hurt!"

It was a losing battle, and Ann knew it. Both Jeremy and Robert wanted to do it *all*. They wanted to play every game that transpired at nearby Edgewood Field and hunt every animal that lived in the deep woods. And it simply wasn't in her to keep saying no. So before she knew it, both of them were playing football too.

Yes, she worried about the way her family was drifting away from church attendance as sports made greater demands—practices, games, team activities. There would be moments when she wondered if they hadn't joined the church of sports, trading a steeple for a goal or a batting cage. But she had to rely on what her heart told her, on Christian training in the home, and on faith that the Lord would work it all out.

Jeremy had been a gift from God at birth; she now felt that he needed a certain gift from his mother.

I'm trusting you on this, Lord, she prayed. *I believe I'm doing the right thing. Please don't let me make a terrible mistake.*

In the end, she gave him the gift of her blessing—her blessing to go out and shine, her blessing to do the things that gave him the deepest joy. In the movie *Chariots of Fire*, Olympic runner Eric Liddell said, "I believe God made me for a purpose, but he also made me fast. And when I run, I feel His pleasure."[1]

Ann Williams trusted that this would be true for her son, that his gifts had a purpose under heaven.

Years later Jeremy would say, "Football took me away from God for a little while, then it brought me back." Sports did rule his heart for a season—no denying that. But his mother would live to see the day when her decision was richly validated. A gift of the heart can expand beyond its intent.

What Ann did for Jeremy turned out to be a blessing to Jeremy's dad, as well. She would realize later how much quality time the father and his sons spent together as a result of her decision. When John Williams passed away at fifty—far too young an age—she was deeply gratified by that realization.

She also knew that the gift didn't stop there. The time would come when a great many other people would be inspired by Jeremy's story, which was made possible, in part, by a mother's gift.

3

BOY MEETS GIRL

IT WAS ONE OF THOSE LATE-NIGHT CHATS THAT HAPPEN only at girls' sleepovers. Jennifer Bolles, a tenth-grader at Shaw High School, sat and looked through yearbook photos with a close friend. There was no shortage of either popcorn or giggles.

They turned the pages and scoped out the cute boys, comparing notes. Jennifer had been on a few dates, but no lasting relationships. No boy in Columbus, in the United States, or in the Milky Way galaxy could escape the shadow of the great monument that had stood in her heart since eighth grade. The massive figure wore a baseball jacket and held a container of Wite-Out.

"C'mon, Jennifer—look at all these boys! You've got to have a crush in here somewhere!"

"Well, not really. I mean, I'm not saying that I wouldn't go out on a date with some of them but . . ."

"Okay, then, let's play it this way. If you could choose any boy, any boy anywhere—I don't care if it's a movie star—who would be your dream date?"

The answer came without delay. "Jeremy Williams."

"Who?"

Jennifer laughed. "Oh, you don't know him. Actually, I don't either! I've had a crush on him *forever*, but he goes to Kendrick so it would be a miracle if I ever got the chance to date him."

She didn't know for sure that Jeremy went to Kendrick. But she guessed he did, because of the direction he'd walked home from middle school two years ago. And she guessed he played baseball because of that jacket he always wore.

Jennifer had known that after eighth grade, their paths would diverge—hers to Shaw, his to rival Kendrick. But in ninth grade, there had been a fresh Jeremy sighting. One spring afternoon the principal had announced over the PA system that Shaw would be taking on Kendrick in baseball that afternoon—on the Shaw field.

Jennifer's ears had perked up. *Kendrick. Baseball.* There was no way that boy was going to set foot on her campus without her being there to see it, so after school she'd crept up into the stands to take a peek.

That wasn't Jeremy on the pitcher's mound. None of the infielders were him either. Left field, center, right—could it be that Jeremy Williams wasn't a ballplayer after all?

Then the catcher threw off his mask and went after a pop foul. It was him! He hadn't gotten much growth, but she still found him adorable.

Sophomore year, after the late-night conversation at the slumber party, she watched him at another baseball game. It was getting to be something of a tradition. Maybe someday he would grow old, retire, and be inducted into the Baseball Hall of Fame in Cooperstown, New York, and she could travel up there and watch him furtively from the crowd. At this rate, he would still have no idea she existed.

Then, junior year, the turning point arrived. Though neither of them would realize it for some time, both of their lives would be changed by the events of the evening.

This time Shaw's basketball teams—boys and girls—traveled across town to play at Kendrick. Jennifer was on the girls' team. After that game was over, she sat in the stands to watch the boys play. She was sitting with her good friend, Leigh, a senior, when the gym door opened and none other than Jeremy Williams walked in.

Jennifer poked Leigh in the ribs. "Look! There he is—look!"

"Who?" asked Leigh, her head swiveling side to side. "What are you talking about?"

"Right there—the one who looks like Tom Cruise. That's Jeremy Williams! I've had a crush on him since the eighth grade!"

"Are you kidding?" asked Leigh. "Go over and talk to him! What's wrong with you?"

"I'd rather die!"

"Well, then, I'll go talk to him for you."

"And you won't be my friend anymore! Leigh, I'm serious!"

The odd thing was, Jeremy didn't settle down. He kept going out the door, then coming back in a few minutes later. Why was he so restless? It would be some time before Jennifer solved this little mystery.

But what mattered most at the moment was that Leigh was now on the case. When summer came, the two friends ran into each other at a New Kids on the Block concert. The boy band was then at the peak of its popularity. "Jennifer!" Leigh called out, pushing her way through the crowd. "I've been wanting to talk to you, girl!"

Jennifer gave her friend, who had graduated in the spring, a big hug. Leigh was grinning like the Cheshire cat. "Guess what I can do?" she asked. "*I* can get *you* a date with Jeremy Williams."

Jennifer's eyes widened. "Get out of town!" she cried, shoving her friend. "No way you can do that!" Then she grabbed her arms and pulled her back. "How can you do that?"

"Because I'm dating his best friend," laughed Leigh.

The Longest Two Weeks in the History of the World

Leigh had taken a summer job at a Winn-Dixie grocery store not far from Kendrick High. There she had met and begun to date Tripp Busby, who was indeed one of Jeremy's best friends. One day she looked out to the parking lot in time to see the driver's door opening from a red pickup truck. *Well, dang,* Leigh thought. *That's him—that's the guy Jennifer likes.*

Sure enough, Jeremy came into the store to visit his buddy, and Leigh made sure she got introduced. Now, she told Jennifer— now she had the power to make magic happen. "How long have you been mooning over that guy? *Years,* right? You've got to let me do this, Jenny. Just think—we could go on double dates for the rest of the summer."

"Girl—"

"No arguments! Tripp and I are already on it, and here's how we have it mapped out. You know you've got county physicals next month, right?"

At the time, Muscogee County required all athletes to undergo physicals just before the year started. It so happened that Shaw would be hosting the procedures this year. In August, all county high school athletes from ten schools, including Kendrick, would be there. Shaw, as the host, would send its kids through the line last. Kendrick would be just before them in line. So Leigh and Tripp had hatched a foolproof plan. Tripp would get Jeremy to the end of his group, and Jennifer would lead the next group. Then, assuming Jennifer didn't go into hiding, nature would take its course.

Jennifer's friend Kathy, who was working at the sign-in table, chose to help nature along a little. When Jeremy walked by, Kathy said, "I know someone who would really like to go out with you." Jennifer wanted to be on the other side of the world somewhere. Or did she?

Jennifer stooped to put her shoes back on after stepping off the scales. Trying to tie her shoestrings, she noticed a pair of Docksides walking toward her. She knew that walk. All of a sudden her hands would not cooperate. As she fumbled with the laces, Jeremy Williams stopped in front of her and said, "Hey, I haven't seen you in a while."

Jeremy leaned over and picked up her papers. Jennifer, giving up on the shoelaces, stood quickly and smiled. A massive frog had lodged in her throat. "Oh, hi," she managed to croak as Jeremy handed her the papers.

Jeremy, on the other hand, was Joe Cool. "You like Shaw?" he asked.

"Yeah. Uh-huh. You, um, you like Kendrick?"

"Yeah." Jeremy smiled. Jennifer tried not to melt.

As they began walking toward the next station, Jennifer was conscious of her shoestrings flapping in the wind. "Well, I guess I'll see you later," Jeremy said.

Jennifer, turning to leave, said to herself, "Definitely!"

Leigh believed it was a done deal. "Oh, yeah, he's interested, girl," she said. "He's fixing to ask you out any day now."

Jennifer spent the next two weeks sitting by the telephone. This being summer, every evening offered some opportunity to be somewhere other than home. She could have gone to the mall with friends, had a swim, or gone horseback riding. But her life right then was all about being there for that phone call.

So she waited. Then she waited some more. And grew more frustrated as the days went by.

What she hadn't taken into account was that Jeremy was not just a baseball player, but a football player. August was the time for two-a-days—a double serving of grueling practices in the August heat and humidity. Players go through drills, run, hit, and sweat off double-digit pounds under their pads and helmets. It's a summer boot camp meant to toughen the team for the season.

In recent years, high school coaches have become more safety conscious, taking precautions to prevent heat exhaustion and heatstroke among the players. But this was the late eighties. The players pushed themselves to the limit. At the end of the day, they went home, replenished their fluids, and collapsed in comatose sleep. There wasn't a lot of energy left for planning the social calendar.

But Jennifer wasn't thinking about two-a-days. All she knew was that the home phone didn't ring unless it was her brother John's girlfriend calling him. *What is taking him so long?* Jennifer wondered.

Finally the phone rang. "Hi, Jennifer, this is Jeremy." *At last.*

Jennifer said hello, asked how he'd been, and they began to chat. Jennifer was thrilled to finally be talking to him. But something seemed different. She couldn't be certain, because she hardly knew him, but he seemed a little too cocky and direct. He said, "Hey, Jennifer, I know your brother. He's a *really* cool guy."

"What?" asked Jennifer. "But how could you—"

Then she figured the whole thing out.

"John! I am going to kill you!" she yelled at the caller, who, of course, was her brother, disguising his voice. "Don't you ever do this again!"

John laughed uproariously while she sputtered and spat out threats. "Hey, I'm just rehearsing you, Jen," he said. "Trying to get you ready for the big phone call with your dream man."

The waiting finally wore on Jennifer. She couldn't stay cloistered away forever, so she finally went out one evening. Her dad greeted her when she arrived at home, and they talked for a few minutes. Then he added, "Oh, yeah—you got a phone call."

"*What?* Why didn't you *tell* me, Dad? Was it—"

"Uh-huh. It was that boy you're always talking about. Jeremy whatever."

Jennifer wanted to scream. She wanted to fire her whole family.

"He took it pretty well," added her dad.

Jennifer whirled around. "Took *what*, Dad? Took *what*?"

"Well, I clowned around with him a little. Like I do, you know."

"*You didn't!*"

"Just having fun."

"Dad, he'll probably never call me back!"

Jennifer's father had a very active sense of humor. As it turned out, so did Jeremy, and he had gotten a kick out of the conversation. At that moment, though, Jennifer wasn't sure how much more of this high-tension craziness she could take.

The next night, a Friday, Jeremy called again. Jennifer answered, and somehow there was a normal conversation. They decided to go see a movie together.

After she hung up, the phone immediately rang—John's girlfriend, Dawn. Jennifer, spiked with adrenalin, brought her up to speed.

"So what do you think, Jenny? What do you think about Jeremy?" asked Dawn.

"Girl, I am going to *marry* that man," said Jennifer.

It was a bold statement. During previous years, Jennifer had her feelings hurt twice by other boys. Just a few months earlier, she'd been lying in her room weeping after having her heart broken, as only a teenage girl can. She had wondered if she should just swear off romance forever. Instead, she'd simply prayed. *Lord, I'm going to give my dating life to you. The next time I date anyone, it's going to be your choice, not mine.*

Within a matter of days, she had seen Leigh at the concert. She'd found out that somehow her good friend was dating Jeremy's best friend. What were the chances of that?

Jennifer sat looking at the phone now, thinking it all through. This was the one boy she'd felt God had made a place for in her heart, even before she knew that place was reserved for him—all the way back in the eighth grade. She had grown up believing in a knight in shining armor who would whisk her away to their castle. In her eyes, somehow, Jeremy had always been that knight.

Now, just before her senior year of high school, a date with Jeremy Williams seemed like a powerful answer to prayer. But would things work out? She really didn't know Jeremy. She didn't know if he was a good person, if he believed in God, or if he would treat her any differently than those other boys had.

She only knew what she had prayed, what her heart said, and what she intended to do: find out who this knight truly was.

The Courtship

The first date was not a roaring success.

They had decided to go see the latest Michael J. Fox movie. They both liked Fox, who had starred in *Back to the Future* and the TV show *Family Ties*. But this one, called *Casualties of War*, wasn't exactly made for a first date. It is a war film and features some stomach-churning scenes of cruelty. Jeremy actually apologized for the content of the movie. Still, they enjoyed each other, and Jeremy asked her out again.

The second date was to a football game, Shaw at Central High over in Phenix City. Jeremy's team was off that week, so he and his friends wanted to scout their opposition. Walking to the stadium, Jeremy reached out and took Jennifer's hand as they crossed a busy street—for him, a casual gesture; for her, a million-dollar moment.

He kept holding her hand as they found the other Kendrick players in the stands. It seemed to Jennifer that Jeremy was showing her off to his friends, parading her by each one as he made introductions. Then, as he talked football with them during the game, he was careful not to ignore her even for a minute—he found ways to include her. He patiently explained football strategy when necessary. He treated her as though she were a valuable gift, something to be cherished. She felt like a princess.

They could have been at a football game or a lecture on nuclear physics. It didn't matter to Jennifer, because of whom she was with. She felt she could relax and simply be herself because Jeremy was so relaxed, so natural. He wasn't out to impress anyone. Jennifer loved everything about him, and prayed, *Lord, thank you for letting him be the person I always thought he was!*

In very short order, Jeremy and Jennifer were more than an item. Even going to different schools, they were all but inseparable.

It helped that she fit in so well with Jeremy's family and he fit in with hers. As time went on, many of their dates involved simply hanging out at each other's homes. Early on, John Williams took his son aside and said, "Jeremy, she's a keeper." His pet name for her was "Skinny Girl."

Ann Williams loved Jennifer too. Ann was devoted to animals, and Jennifer was particularly into horses. As for Jeremy's sister, Kimberly immediately felt she had a new sister. Jennifer seemed more genuine than other girls who had come around in pursuit of her brother. They were nice to her to win bonus points with Jeremy, while Jennifer actually spent time hanging out with Kimberly, helping her with basketball, doing girl stuff.

The Bolles household felt the same way about Jeremy. They were curious to see this boy who had so enchanted Jennifer all these years. He might be quiet, but his easy way and sense of humor went down well with the Bolles family. It was also clear that he had a level head, was a hard worker, and knew where he was going in life. He made top grades in school, belonged to the National Honor Society, starred in athletics—what wasn't there to like?

Jennifer's dreams would seem to have come true, her prayers answered. Senior year was going to be great. It seemed to her that God's timing was perfect.

She had no idea just how perfect that timing was when it came to Jeremy's life.

4

FINDING FOCUS

SWEET SIXTEEN. REALLY? IT ALL DEPENDS UPON YOUR PER-spective.

If you're a sixteen-year-old boy, there are many things that are sweet about sixteen, starting with the acquisition of a driver's license. That little rectangle of laminated plastic is a personal ticket to freedom, to mobility—places to go and friends to see.

Sixteen also usually means becoming an upperclassman at high school. Navigating the rough waters of adolescence, you receive your first green glimpse of the approaching continent of adulthood. Puberty is almost complete, and if you're lucky you may even find a few hairs sprouting on your chest. Your height increases. Your voice is comfortably deeper, no longer squeaking back into the soprano range at the most embarrassing times. And psychologists tell us that there's a spike in mental and reasoning abilities at this juncture, so you may also become more confident in your debating skills—particularly when your parents are the opponents.

Up to now, life has been family dominated. But now you

begin to see the world outside your home. Friends become your focus. You want to be more independent, to form your own opinions, to find your own niche in the world. It's a time of dizzying excitement for you and inevitable anxiety for your parents. But it's normal and probably necessary.

Jeremy Williams at sixteen would have made any parent proud. He was an A and B student, a member of the National Honor Society, a polite and cooperative young man who kept his life and his language clean. When he wasn't studying, he was at practice or otherwise involved in sports. And when he wasn't doing that, he was hunting or fishing or catching up on his sleep. He was the proverbial all-American boy.

But nobody moves through this period of life without rocking the boat just a little. It's normal, and to an extent it's even healthy. At this age, Jeremy experienced what he would later call his "year of rebellion."

The focal point of his acting out was his relationship with his parents—a traditional, loving mother and father who were intent on keeping their son on the right path. In particular, Ann Williams had an intense hatred of alcohol. She knew that kids of a certain age were likely to experiment with it, and she also knew it could become a gateway to a devastated life. She had seen that happen among relatives and friends, nearly losing someone she loved due to alcohol.

"This will not happen in our house," she'd vowed.

The Seventh-day Adventist Church fully endorsed her views on drinking. As many other Christian denominations softened their stances, Ann's church held the line against alcohol, tobacco, and narcotics.

On at least one occasion, Jeremy came home from a party

and tried to breeze past his mother to his room. But she recognized the signs—and the aroma. Ann marched her son out to his truck, rooted through it until she found the bottle, and poured out the rest of the liquor as he watched. "This will not happen," she said.

Ann, the worrier, lost a lot of sleep in those days. "What if he follows the wrong crowd?" she asked her husband late at night. "What if he becomes really wild?"

"Trust your son," said John. "You know how we've raised him. You know who he is. It'll work out."

Ann insisted upon high standards in other areas too. She was still enforcing a nine-thirty bedtime on her sixteen-year-old. She wanted to know where her son was and who he was with at all times. She offered advisories as he went out the door and smelled his breath as he came back in. Ann was loving and never unfair, but when a child reaches sixteen, some pushback is inevitable. Peer pressure is strong. "Years of rebellion" happen. The difference comes in how they're handled.

Jeremy couldn't help feeling a little stifled by all the rules. After all, he had always kept his nose clean. Like any teenager, he had questions about life, about right and wrong, and about what kind of person he wanted to be. He tested the boundaries, getting into significant trouble exactly once. But that one time was frightening, humiliating, and life-altering. It was enough to create a serious threat to his future, enough to sound a harsh alarm in his heart and soul. Jeremy received a terrible glimpse of how little is required to disrupt a promising young man's life and destroy his dreams.

If Jeremy had questions about where he wanted to go with his life, this experience suggested a few answers.

ONE JANUARY NIGHT

Friday evening, January 6, 1989.

So many things came together that night.

The first of them was rather innocuous: it was Ann's birthday. Her son would present her with a strange gift indeed, one of the last things in the world she desired. Yet in the great scheme of things, it turned out to be a blessing in a fairly ugly disguise.

The second of those things was that Jennifer Bolles happened to be at a basketball game in which Kendrick hosted Shaw. She also happened to look up just in time to see Jeremy Williams enter the gymnasium and then to tell her friend Leigh about it. This was indeed the very evening that eventually made it possible for Jeremy and Jennifer to enter each other's lives. Jeremy just wasn't aware of it at the time.

The third of those things involved the reason Jeremy kept moving in and out the door of the gym. He was, in fact, sharing a bottle with a few of his buddies out in the parking lot. It's a ritual as old as high school athletics: someone sneaks an item from his father's liquor cabinet, and his friends huddle furtively in the shadows, taking swigs.

This was exactly the kind of thing Ann didn't want to happen—and on her birthday, no less. But it wasn't so much the alcohol that ultimately changed lives. It was what happened next.

The group ultimately left the game, adjourning to a pool hall known as Clicks. It was in a little strip mall, across the street from the Adventist church. At Clicks, three of the guys got into a conversation about an event that infuriated them. One of them had a girlfriend who was a cheerleader, but the cheerleader coach, a teacher at Kendrick, had benched her from cheering during a basketball game. Jeremy and his friends saw this as an act of intentional humiliation in front of the whole student body. Such a thing could not stand, as they saw it. So on this Friday night, with the limited inhibitions a few drinks can afford, they decided to do something.

The teacher happened to live nearby, just across the street and down the block. Soon, in the early hours of Saturday morning, they were in her driveway with a can of spray paint. They applied splotches of the new color to her car, then disappeared under the cover of darkness.

For Jeremy, one of the worst things about the ensuing weeks was the constant tension. Jeremy had never been in trouble before. He kept thinking about the act they had perpetrated. It was just as his mother had told him so many times—nothing good comes from late nights and drinking.

What if someone finds out? he thought. *Will I be expelled? Lose my truck? Get kicked off the team?*

The teacher, it turned out, was married to a police officer. This did nothing to help the matter go away. The Columbus police were all but convinced that a student or a group of them—was behind the act of vandalism. And they were asking lots of questions of students, teachers, and parents.

Jeremy had heard a Bible verse quoted at church sometime or other, from the book of Numbers, chapter 32: "You may be sure that your sin will find you out" (v. 23). Now that verse seemed like a warning. And sure enough, one of the boys talked. He bragged to a buddy or two, and, of course, those friends had to tell others. Secrets have a way of liberating themselves. They're made to go viral.

Ann noticed that Jeremy had become very quiet the past few weeks as spring approached. He ambled up to her two or three times, trying to say something. But it was all very vague—something about the police asking questions. He wouldn't look her in the eye. Maybe, he suggested, she would hear something from them. It sounded odd, but Ann had a hard time believing any police business could possibly be connected to her son.

Then, of course, it all came out. The police made it known they were going to bring in Jeremy and his friends. As a matter of fact, they were planning to arrest him in the middle of a big baseball game at the Columbus State University field. A bit of lobbying went on, however, and the police agreed to handle things more discreetly.

Jeremy hadn't been the prime instigator, though Ann recognized the spray paint color from a can on her own shelf. Still, he was the oldest of the three boys and the best known, so the police and the victim assumed he must be the ringleader. He took the brunt of the punishment.

The coaches and others in the community spoke up for Jeremy. They pointed out that his was a true first-time offense and that this was a great kid, a positive figure in the school and community who had slipped up while intoxicated and made one bad mistake. But the teacher with the spray-painted car wasn't going to let it all go so easily. She wanted to press charges, putting the crime on Jeremy's permanent record so that no college would look at him.

Cooler heads ultimately prevailed. Jeremy and the others had to pay a nice sum of restitution and put in many hours of community service. To him they were small prices to pay compared with the weeks of guilt, anxiety, and deep concern that he had put a great hole in his future—plus the public humiliation.

There could have been no more effective way to put a final exclamation mark on Jeremy Williams's "year of rebellion."

"If you ever give me another birthday present like that one, you won't live to go to jail," his mother told him. "I'll kill you myself!"

Meanwhile, across town, Jennifer Bolles was completely oblivious to these developments. She had seen Jeremy in the last moments before her shining knight got his armor dirty, but it was all the same to her.

The world seemed to take an extra turn on that night in January—though, amazingly, the two of them never compared notes on the two separate incidents until 2012, while preparing this book. Until then, neither had realized that the spray-painting incident and the appearance that eventually got them together had happened at the same time.

It felt like the fingerprints of God.

A Time for Reflection

Spring should have been brighter, happier. It was the time for baseball and nice weather and finishing another school semester. Instead, a dark cloud hung over the last months of Jeremy's junior year.

Summer brought the quiet after that storm. Jeremy worked hard, paid his share of restitution, finished his community service, and spent a lot of time thinking. He'd had his taste of being the "bad boy," the kid people whisper about as he walks by. He might be many things, but he just wasn't cut out to be a rebel. Maybe he'd been tired of being the golden boy, but the other extreme was no option at all.

Then, during the summer, Jeremy's friend Tripp began talking to him about some girl, Leigh's friend, who supposedly had a crush on him. Well, that was just what he needed. Girls had come after him before, but he really hadn't had time for dating. The way he saw it, girls attached themselves to you, established ownership over your life, and whined whenever you wanted to go hunting for the weekend.

But Tripp kept after him about this one girl, and maybe it was time for new things. He actually remembered this Jennifer Bolles—not too well, just a face from junior high days—but he did remember her. So he was a little curious. Once he caught sight of her at the school physicals, he liked the way she looked too.

From there, of course, things went very well. They talked, they went out, they went out again. Jennifer was nothing like he'd expected. The only word he had for her was *real*. She didn't put on a show for him. She didn't tease or flirt. It was very clear that she liked him—a lot—but there were no games, no foolishness, no attempts to gain control over his life. She fit in with his buddies and his family, and she actually dug sports.

When he was with her, he felt happy and at ease. Comfortable. And when he wasn't, he was finding that he missed her company. She was a good person, through and through, and it felt good to be with someone like that after his experiences during the previous year.

A steady girlfriend was something very new for Jeremy and the last thing he expected, coming into the home stretch of his high school days. But something about it just seemed right.

They dated through the fall, and he even began attending church with her family at Edgewood Baptist Church. Sunday services, of course, were new to him. That simply hadn't been an option in his household. Jeremy liked being able to worship while still being involved in the activities that meant so much to him.

As Jeremy sat in the quiet sanctuary—a little older, a little wiser, still a little wounded from "Spray-gate"—he was able to reflect on what was important in his life. He had been raised in a Christian home, but now he could think about faith with a little more maturity and a better sense of what it really meant to him. He found himself reflecting on other verses he'd heard growing up: "When I was a child, I talked like a child, I thought like a child, I reasoned like a child. When I became a man, I put the ways of childhood behind me" (1 Cor. 13:11).

This verse summed up how he was feeling these days. The grown-up realities of college and adulthood were almost upon him, and he was ready. His childhood had been almost perfect—wonderful family, incredible neighborhood filled with friends, and so much opportunity to do the things he loved. He'd had his little walk on the wild side, and he knew that wasn't who he was.

For the first time, he was ready to think serious thoughts—*future* thoughts. More and more, those thoughts included God—and Jennifer too.

It was nice to put away the childish things.

ALL THE INTANGIBLES

By the time Jeremy's senior year began, his best sport had become obvious. He loved them all, including golf. But he was passionate about football.

He still didn't have the big, durable frame that lends itself to the game, but he made up for that in mind and spirit. Jeremy was relentlessly driven, never loafing during a play, his motor never stopping until the whistle blew. Just as important, he was a student of the discipline of football. He studied game film, did his homework, and got himself into position to predict what the other team was going to do.

As a senior, Jeremy played quarterback on offense and safety on defense, excelling on both sides of the ball. Coach David Taylor, who was Kendrick's offensive coordinator until Jeremy's senior season, remembers him as a hardworking, blue-collar-type athlete who was the consummate team player. Jeremy wasn't the type to steal the limelight. He was all about Kendrick winning every game.

"He may not have been big, but . . . he wasn't fast either," Coach Taylor laughs. "Jeremy Williams wasn't that much of a physical specimen. But I'll never forget what he did about that. He ran speed drills on his own, anything that might help him get a little faster, a little quicker. He ran up and down those steep slopes that Kendrick has. And he got himself one of those parachutes you can run with—the kind that isn't as big as an airplane chute, but you run with it on, the air catches it, and you fight the resistance."

With all that work, Jeremy brought his forty-yard-dash speed down to a very respectable 4.5 seconds, an eye-popping improvement. He got into the weight room and built up his strength. *Build it and they'll come,* he told himself—build the body, increase the speed, work your tail off, and the college scouts will come. Jeremy had his sights set on a scholarship. But even during his stellar senior season, coaches from the best college football factories never showed any interest. For that matter, neither did most of the smaller ones.

Coach Taylor had taken another position by this time—at Jennifer's high school, Shaw—but he remembers talking to a visiting coach from a Division I college. They went over some of the better prospects at Shaw, and then the recruiter said, "Hey, I have one other question for you. You had this kid over at Kendrick, didn't you? This defensive back?"

"Jeremy Williams—I sure did."

"What can you tell me about him?"

"I'll tell you this," said Coach Taylor. "He's a big hitter. He never takes plays off. He's a great kid and a good student who will make all your other players better, because he knows the game as well as most of the coaches."

"Okay, sounds impressive. How big is he?"

"Well, not very. His height is five-ten, and he probably weighs 175. [Coach Taylor was being generous.] But you know, this is one of those players with all the intangibles."

"Oh well, thanks for the info." The light had gone out of the recruiter's eyes, and Coach Taylor could see that he couldn't get beyond the "measurables," the height and weight that the big schools expect.

Coach Taylor said, "Let me just say this to you. Give me a team full of Jeremy Williams types, and you can have all the six-two, 240-pound kids. I'll take my blue-collar kids and whip your blue-chip recruits with 'em."

The visitor laughed and went on his way. His school didn't recruit Jeremy. Neither did most of the others.

Only one Division I coach showed up with an offer, in fact, and it happened because of a legendary game against yet another cross-town rival.

THE BATTLE OF COLUMBUS

Baker High was a historic school that stood proudly in the shadow of Fort Benning from the time of World War II until a fire destroyed much of the building in 2010. (Newt Gingrich was a Baker alumnus.) And the rivalry between Baker High and Kendrick was nearly as historic. In the late 1980s, when Jeremy was a student, the Kendrick-Baker games were renowned for their ferocity. And their clash in the fall of 1989, his senior year, promised to be one of those all-out wars that no one forgets.

The two head coaches, Howard "Buzz" Busby for Kendrick (Tripp Busby's dad) and Dan Ragle for Baker, had been hired by their respective schools on the same day two years earlier. The teams were evenly matched and driven to beat one another. The fact that Kendrick had to win the game to make the play-offs upped the ante.

The game was played at Memorial Stadium in downtown Columbus. Fans who expected an intense, hard-hitting battle were not disappointed. And Jeremy Williams had the game of his high school career that night, playing quarterback on offense and safety on defense, the leader on the field for both units.

He started the game with a huge hit in the end zone that caused a Baker interception; he finished the game by triggering a Baker fumble to preserve the victory. Jeremy compiled five solo tackles, three shared ones, three pass breakups, and two interceptions in a tight 7–0 win. Coach Busby would later recall that Jeremy "left the field with bloodshot eyes, a crust of mud on his face and a facemask so mangled that we had to throw it away."[1]

A mangled face mask is no ordinary sight at any level of football. Many of these "helmet cages" are constructed with lightweight stainless steel. Automobile bumpers are often dented, but not face masks. But it happened that night. Jeremy was hitting so hard, pursuing so relentlessly, and taking such vicious tackles on offense that he ended up with a broken nose as well. He had to stand and complete a pass for a first down with a defensive end closing in on him; he took the blow and made the play.

He wouldn't have minded the broken nose so much if his brother's wedding weren't the following day. He had to appear as a groomsman in that wedding with a mangled nose that the mangled mask had failed to protect. He also had to take the SAT standardized test before the wedding.

Months later, Coach Busby was asked to describe Jeremy in one word. He thought for a moment and then answered, "Tenacious." A tenacious person is determined and fiercely persistent. It's someone with a firm grip, who stands firm and holds fast.

It was a description that would follow Jeremy all his life.

He may not have looked his best in the wedding pictures, but what counted was how he looked on the game film. Providentially, it fell into the hands of a college coach named Joe Lee Dunn.

Through a colorful career, Dunn has coached at schools all over the country, including New Mexico, South Carolina, Ole Miss, Arkansas, and Mississippi State. In 1989, however, he was defensive coordinator of the school then known as Memphis State (now the University of Memphis). He was a Columbus native himself, so he had a lot of pipeline connections to the athletic talent in the city. One of these was an old mentor, Joe Sparks, who had been at the game. Sparks put the tape in the mail to Memphis, Tennessee, with the instructions: "Watch the Kendrick safety."

Dunn watched, and he liked what he saw.

Tough, uncompromising, and homespun, Dunn was known among fans for his aversion to wearing socks and among opposing coaches for destroying their offensive game plans. Joe Lee

Dunn believed in a pressure defense, technically known as a 3-3-5, designed to confuse and intimidate those who lined up against it. Many head coaches of superior teams ended up hiring Joe Lee Dunn to coach their defense because it was so hard to beat him on the other side of the field.

One of these, former Kentucky coach Hal Mumme, said, "Joe Lee beats you on Tuesday. You play on Saturday, but on the Tuesday before it, you've got your kids trying to pick all this stuff up. By the time they get to the game, their heads are messed up."[2]

In particular, Coach Dunn's defenses needed smart, hustling, talented players—playmakers—in the defensive secondary. And in the Kendrick-Baker game film, he found one. Everything about Jeremy's game film impressed him. Size didn't seem to matter when you saw him hit. Speed didn't seem an issue when you saw him get to the ball carrier first, play after play. Jeremy Williams was Dunn's kind of player, a smart gamer with a killer instinct.

When Memphis State offered Jeremy a full academic scholarship, it came as a shock. No other Division I-A school believed in him. He had received letters of interest as an underclassman, but all those schools expected him to come into a growth spurt, as often happens late in high school. It didn't happen for Jeremy, and the letters trailed off. Jeremy's plan was to walk on to the team at Georgia Southern, a smaller I-AA program in Statesboro, and room with his friend Paul Carroll. He would have to pay his tuition, but at least he'd get a chance to play. (Later, after Memphis offered, he would receive offers from West Georgia and Valdosta State.)

But the Memphis State offer changed everything. It seemed impossible to turn down such an opportunity—though Ann had some concerns. Memphis was an eight-hour drive from

Columbus, she pointed out. She couldn't imagine her boy being so far from home. Then again, college education was among her dearest goals for her children, and she regretted that she had discouraged Robert from accepting an offer to play in South Dakota. If you have a chance to go to college, she told Jeremy, you need to take it. If Jeremy wanted to go to Memphis, he could go with her blessing.

Jeremy made plans to sign his letter of intent with Memphis State in February, at a special local ceremony at the Western Sizzlin restaurant. He would play football for the MSU Tigers and get the best education he could. The future couldn't have been brighter—particularly after what had happened in his life only a month earlier, just before New Year's Day.

COMING FORWARD

They were both seniors. This would be their only high school Christmas together. So Jennifer asked Jeremy for a special gift. She wanted him to accompany her to an all-day youth event in Macon, Georgia, sponsored by the Southern Baptist Convention. The event, which was scheduled for the week between Christmas and New Year's, would feature plenty of music by Christian bands and teaching by special speakers. Jeremy and Jennifer boarded a rowdy bus full of teenagers for a ride down Highway 80 to the Macon Coliseum and a full day of Christian celebration.

The music was outstanding. The speakers were funny and engaging. More important, the speakers were challenging—and *challenge* had always been the key word for motivating Jeremy. He responded to compelling invitations to take on great goals. Good coaches challenged him. Gifted teachers challenged him.

And on that December day a minister of the gospel offered him the greatest challenge of his life.

The speaker gave a clear presentation of what it meant to be a devoted follower of Jesus Christ. God, he explained, is holy and just in his dealings with sin. Yet he is also loving and forgiving, a Father who longs to gather in his lost children, to bless them in this life and give them a home in the next life.

Unfortunately, the man explained, our sin gets in the way. Jeremy knew this from painful experience: *your sin shall find you out.* So often he worried about God's anger, God's punishment. He knew there were plenty of things in his life that must displease the Lord.

But after the recent months of attending church with Jennifer and now hearing this speaker, he was seeing God in a different light. He really liked the speaker's depiction of a loving, forgiving heavenly Father. It made him think of his own father, whose love was his greatest attribute. *If my father in this world is so loving,* Jeremy thought, *how much more loving and patient is my Father in heaven?*

The speaker went on to explain how useless it is for us to try to be "good enough" people—to strain to measure up to God's standards on our own feeble efforts. No matter how hard we try, no matter how pure our intentions, we stumble. We become entangled in the sin that is born into us. The best people in the world are sinners. None of them can please God on their own.

That made sense to Jeremy too. He thought about his life as a top student, a top athlete, an obedient son—all of that—and knew something was missing. He was sure of it. He'd had so many advantages and tried so hard to do the right thing, yet he still had been capable of the rebellion that disrupted his junior year.

Then the speaker came to the edge of the stage and spoke quietly, intently. It felt as if there was no one in the audience but Jeremy, and every word was targeted toward his heart alone.

"Jesus is a bridge to all the joy and peace you've longed for. He is God's way of bringing you home," the man said. "*You* can't get across that deep canyon. *I* can't get across it. We'd be helpless and fall to our death. But Jesus is the bridge. His cross spans the gap, reaching from the heaven he has for you to where you are right now.

"Jesus does it this way: He takes the punishment for your sins. The punishment you can't afford to take. He hung on that cross thinking of you, saying, 'Father, forgive Jeremy, for he knows not what he does.'" (This was how Jeremy heard it, a message just for him.)

"Don't you feel that today is your day?" the speaker asked. "Don't you want to walk across that bridge that Jesus has made for you? You'll be forgiven. You'll live forever. But more important, you'll live *better*. Right now—today—then tomorrow and the rest of your life. You'll live for *him*. You'll do everything for his glory, and it will make all the difference."

Then, as the musicians came to their instruments and began to play, the man invited those in his audience to be courageous— to stand up, walk down the aisle, and pray with a youth counselor. Jeremy heard that invitation as a challenge and he didn't hesitate for an instant. Nothing had ever seemed more clear.

He reached over, took Jennifer's hand, and pulled her up with him. He tugged her into the aisle, and the two of them began walking toward the platform.

Jennifer had committed her life to Christ as a child. But it was different for Jeremy. He had the training she did, but for some reason it had never really taken root, never quite clicked in his head and heart. Only now did he have ears to hear the message, eyes to see his need, and a thirst to drink deeply from the living water that was being offered. Now, for the first time, he'd found true, saving faith.

Faith was about exchanging guilt for the joy of forgiveness. Through faith, God would remove punishment for sin and replace it with love.

When Jeremy and Jennifer reached the platform, a counselor stepped forward, embraced the two of them, and led them to a stairwell. There she talked with them for a few minutes, then helped Jeremy pray to receive Christ. Tears ran down Jennifer's face as she listened to Jeremy's prayer.

Jeremy left the rally exhilarated and energized. He knew what his life was about now. He knew that he could continue to be a student, but that he would be a student for the glory of God. He would continue to play competitive sports, but he would play for Christ rather than himself. Everything was going to be different.

Jeremy had been through a tumultuous year. He felt like he'd been to the depths of the valley, then the top of the mountain, in just fifty-one weeks. Against all odds, he had won a scholarship to a good college. He had found a girl he truly loved. A year ago, he had made choices that could have stripped his life of all these possibilities. Now, through Christ, all things were possible.

On the bus ride home, he couldn't stop smiling. Neither could Jennifer as she clutched his hand and put her head on his shoulder. What a day, and what an amazing way to start a new year—and a new life.

5

THE LEGEND OF THE GEORGIA ASSASSIN

Jennifer thought she might never stop crying.

It was February of 1990—just another weekday at Shaw High. Kids were chatting at their lockers, laughing, going to class as usual, as if the worst thing in the world weren't happening. What did they care that some senior jock over at Kendrick was signing away four years of his life to a distant city, a place where his face could not be seen, nor his hand held on a daily basis?

She imagined him across town, sitting at a table at Western Sizzlin, flanked by his high school coach Buzz Busby and Joe Lee Dunn of Memphis State University. She imagined his parents and friends applauding and cameras flashing as he placed his signature on a letter of intent to accept a scholarship to play and study at MSU. This was the day it all became signed, sealed, and delivered. And it felt as if her heart was breaking.

Jennifer would love Jeremy no matter where he traveled. After six months together, the two of them were absolutely, unconditionally committed to each other. They both believed

61

what they had was a forever thing. But the distance wasn't going to be easy to take. Jeremy was about to become a voice on a telephone, an ink scrawl on stationery, and a physical presence for holidays and visits only.

Jennifer couldn't help but think about all those years of growing up, so closely together and yet apart. They'd just been dating a few months, and now he was leaving. She knew that God had put it all together, but sometimes his timing was difficult to understand.

Tears kept streaming down Jennifer's cheeks right there in physics class. She couldn't help it. Her friend Clint, who had sat next to her since seventh grade, was deeply concerned. "What's wrong, Jennifer?" he asked.

"Jeremy's going to Memphis," she blubbered. Then, after class, she went to find her mother, who taught at Shaw. "Mom, I'm a mess. I need to go home."

Kathy Bolles gave her a hug and wiped away a few of the tears. "Can you wait until eleven, when you're counted as present? That's only thirty more minutes. Then you can check out." Jennifer had only missed one day of school in her life, other than during a bout with chicken pox. Her mom knew she would be upset later for staining her near-perfect attendance record.

"Cry it out today, baby," Kathy added. "We all love Jeremy and will miss him. But God will see you through this. I'm praying for you."

For the next three months, the couple spent every possible moment together, determined to get the most out of the spring and summer. They attended each other's proms and other events and hung out together on weekends. But time seemed to speed by, and the day came for Jeremy to make that long trek to Memphis.

Jennifer rode up to Tennessee with Jeremy, his parents, and his sister. The route would become very familiar over those years —northwest toward Birmingham and the inevitable restroom and snack stop at McDonald's, then onward through Tupelo, and finally into the southwest corner of Tennessee, where Jeremy would make his new home.

After that first long drive, the Williamses' car pulled up to Jeremy's dorm. When the family went to see the field house, where the coaches would meet the players, a door opened, a great shadow fell across the earth, and a monster stood before them.

He was six-foot-seven and 350 pounds' worth of future NFL offensive lineman, otherwise known as Eduardo Vega. The Williamses had never in their lives seen a human being of any kind so large. Some of the other freshman players came walking out, too, and in no way, shape, or form did they resemble high school players.

"Excuse me," Ann Williams asked one of them, "are you a senior?"

"No ma'am," said the player. "I'm a freshman."

Ann turned around, grabbed Jeremy's arm, and said, "Come on, you're going home."

Everyone laughed, but Ann wasn't so sure she was joking. For years, she had held the line against Jeremy's playing such a dangerous game. She had finally given in, and now he was being thrown into the arena with a bunch of hungry lions.

Jeremy pointed out that, as a safety, he wouldn't be lining up against the bigger guys. He'd be chasing down a bunch of skinny receivers and lightweight scatbacks. Ann wasn't convinced, though she did have to admit that she liked Jeremy's roommate. His name was Brett Whiddon, and he was a fellow Georgia boy—from football-rich Lowndes County. Like Jeremy,

Brett was a free safety. The two of them had a lot in common, and they hit it off quickly. They would room together for three years and become lifelong friends.

Stepping Up

Jennifer and the Williams family had decided to attend all the Memphis State home games. In between games, they kept up with Jeremy through letters and phone calls. He was doing well and had no complaints. College ball was far more demanding than high school, and he was being supremely challenged— which was just the way he liked things.

Arrival at college is an adventure for every freshman who plays Division I ball, and it can definitely feel like a comedown. After all, these kids have usually been the best in the neighborhood, the best in their youth leagues, the best on the high school roster. They have shelves full of all-star trophies. On a major college team, almost everyone has trophies—even many of the walk-ons, those nonscholarship players who practice and help the team prepare for games. Even Jeremy, who wasn't highly recruited, was well known in football circles in his corner of the world.

Freshman recruits arrive on campus as big fish from small ponds. But they're about to be released into an ocean of sharks. College players are bigger, faster, stronger, and they tend to play more complex schemes. The upperclassmen have been working out in high-tech strength and conditioning programs under the guidance of professionals. They also have an irreplaceable advantage: experience. They've had their abilities honed and sharpened to a much finer edge.

A quarterback, for example, may get by with all kinds of idiosyncrasies in high school. On the college campus, he must learn perfect footwork, the right release, and especially the discipline of "reading" the defense. He has to master a far more complex playbook. Blockers and tacklers must start all over again with better fundamentals for their craft.

Jeremy actually had an advantage, in fact, when he arrived at Memphis State. He didn't come in with an enlarged ego. He had received excellent coaching on the high school level, and he understood he was about to take harder hits and harsher, more demanding coaching. He knew it wouldn't be so easy to run down quarterbacks and receivers with elite speed, so he was prepared to train extra hard. And he still had that signature character trait: tenacity. His goals were to give his greatest effort on every single play until the whistle blew, to stand his ground without intimidation, and, of course, to play for Christ and then for his team.

Every fall, when the freshmen show up for college ball, a few hotshots fall by the wayside. Others, less heralded, catch the eye of coaches. Few freshmen start their first game, and a great many accept a "redshirt," meaning they sit out the year and maintain a season of eligibility.

Jeremy made enough of an early impression to make the active roster. He even made the "two-deep," meaning he would back up the starter at his position. But when his parents, his sister, and Jennifer arrived for the opener, a game against Arkansas State, he warned them, "Don't be let down if I never get in. This guy in front of me is *good*."

He knew his people had traveled a great distance to watch him sit on a bench, but they had to realize he wasn't at Kendrick anymore. Memphis State played an ambitious schedule of several Southeastern Conference teams every single year. The Tigers played in the historic Liberty Bowl, a field of dreams where Bo Jackson and Lawrence Taylor and Doug Flutie had run and thrown and tackled. Legends had coached here: Bear Bryant and Lou Holtz and Tom Osborne. It was an honor just to buckle a chin strap in such a place.

On the other hand, Memphis State football had been stuck in neutral for a while. Head coach Chuck Stobart's first team had finished 2–9 the previous season. The second year is always a big one for new coaches, so 1990 needed to be a good one. Practice had been particularly rigorous and demanding, and Jeremy understood that a hungry program presented opportunities for a hungry player—even a young one.

BREAKING OUT

The Williams delegation was all decked out in team colors, pom-poms in hand, wearing large buttons with the number 19, Jeremy's jersey number, plastered across them. It wasn't a number he'd been excited to receive. "Who wants a number like 19?" he moaned. Freshmen get leftovers on jersey digits.

It helped a little to remember great football players who had worn the number. Johnny Unitas, the great Baltimore Colts quarterback, had worn the one-nine. Joe Montana had sported it, but only when he played for Kansas City. For Jeremy, 19 just didn't have that classic ring to it.

"But that's *our* number," Jennifer protested. "Our first date was August 19!"

"Hey, I guess you're right," said Jeremy.

Later, he would be proud to wear 19. Ultimately numbers

only have the meaning we give them. Jeremy and Jennifer would get married on June 19, and the number would retain special significance for them over the years.

Jennifer had brought a huge video camera so she could record all Jeremy's highlights for posterity. But he was predicting a lot of bench sitting, so she decided she might as well catch him on video during pregame stretches.

Football warm-ups are lengthy, and Jennifer captured the whole thing: 19 doing his exercises with everyone else, 19 participating in tip drills and other rituals, 19 running back into the locker room. Kimberly, Jeremy's sister, provided color commentary. The battery light on the camera began to blink, meaning she'd soon be out of juice. But 19 wasn't going to play anyway, right?

Wrong.

On the first play of the second quarter, the Tigers' starting free safety came out of the game with an injured back—and in went his backup, Jeremy Williams. In the defensive huddle, he looked like a pygmy. Most MSU fans probably thought, *We're in big trouble.*

But the Williams delegation began cheering. Jennifer screamed loudest of all and reached for her video camera to enshrine the moment. It clicked lifelessly, and she realized that now, with Jeremy playing his first actual college football, her camera battery was dead.

On his very first play, pumped with adrenalin, Jeremy shot laser straight to the ball carrier and made a crushing, open-field tackle. In the stands, a few eyebrows went up. Jennifer and the Williamses screamed themselves silly.

Memphis State fans weren't known for their passion in the manner of, say, SEC fans. Most Tiger supporters were embarrassed to be tied with the likes of Arkansas State. But the Williams traveling party behaved as if MSU had just won the Super Bowl.

The crowd would become accustomed to the Columbus group. As a matter of fact, soon they were joining the Jeremy Williams cheering section.

Jeremy played very well that day, especially considering he was a raw rookie whose suitcase was barely unpacked. He saw the field as all freshmen see it: everything moving twice as fast as normal, the wide receivers big and strong and able to run like deer. But he held his own. And far from being timid, he actually drew a personal foul at the end of the game. It involved a long, incomplete pass in which he and the receiver both leaped out of bounds, and Jeremy slammed into the other player on the ground, drawing a flag.

It was a tight game, ending in a tie, and the crowd booed the penalty. But Jeremy's group celebrated. "My boyfriend made that hit! That's my boyfriend!" shrieked Jennifer, jumping up and down and pointing out her "19" button to everyone in the section.

Coach Dunn's faith in an undersized player was fully validated. "I don't care so much about his size," he'd said when recruiting Jeremy. "It's his heart that interests me."

PRESSING ON

Once Jeremy left the bench in game one, he never returned to it. He started in seven games at free safety for the rest of his freshman year, appearing in all eleven games. He then started in all thirty-three games the remainder of his four years at Memphis State University. To longtime sports fans, Jeremy's achievement—coming off the bench because of an injury—was reminiscent of a baseball Hall of Famer from another era.

In 1923, the New York Yankees had a young first baseman on the bench, a kid who rarely saw the field. The starter, a player by the name of Wally Pipp, was held out of the lineup one day, though the reasons aren't clear. The kid was inserted at first base, and he never came out, not for many years. He played 2,130 consecutive games, a record that stood for fifty-six years until 1995, when Cal Ripken Jr. broke it.

When the Yankee was finally unable to play, in 1939, it was because of a little-known motor-neuron disease diagnosed by the Mayo Clinic as amyotropic lateral sclerosis (ALS). The player's name, of course, was Lou Gehrig, and he was so beloved by this time that his name became attached to ALS as "Lou Gehrig's disease."

Jeremy's experience of stepping in and holding on, Gehrig-style, established a pleasant parallel between the two athletes. Years later, of course, the parallel would take on a darker aspect.

But in 1990, Jeremy Williams was simply an eighteen-year-old having the time of his life, doing what he felt destined to do, and doing it better than most people expected.

The second week of his college career, he received his first start. It came at Vaught-Hemingway Stadium in Oxford, Mississippi, against the University of Mississippi. This happened to be one of Ole Miss's finest teams under Coach Billy Brewer; they would finish 9–3, with an appearance in the Gator Bowl. Forty-two thousand fans packed the stadium that day, one of the largest crowds in Mississippi history. And Memphis State actually led at halftime.

But Jeremy had been thrown into the arena very early, and occasionally it showed in the game. Some of his overflowing adrenalin had worn off by then, and he'd been hit early and often by massive, crazily athletic human specimens such as he had never seen. Ole Miss quarterback, Russ Shows, threw for nearly 400 yards in the game, at least some of which came at Jeremy's expense.

The coaches loved their new free safety's aggressive nature, but sometimes the very same trait made them crazy. Jeremy was so motivated, so hungry to make the play, that he might bite on a fake during these early games, turning the wrong way and letting a receiver loose or missing his assignment on an option pitch. His teammates later remembered Joe Lee Dunn's voice bellowing from the sidelines: "JerremmyyYYYYY!"

In the final moments of the Ole Miss game, Jeremy and the defense kept battling, hanging on for dear life to a small lead. But they were all but played out by this time; they'd left all they had on the field. Ole Miss completed a ten-play drive to win the game by two points.

The Tigers were distraught in the locker room after the game. They'd been so close to an immense upset victory on the road. It just hadn't been their day.

But their day would come less than a year later.

It turned out to be one of those strange years for Memphis State. They were capable of delivering an inspired performance against a bowl team like Ole Miss, which was ranked as high as fifteenth by the Associated Press during the season. But they were also capable of losing to less talented opponents. Memphis State dropped three in a row at the end, finishing 4–6–1. It was a two-game improvement over the previous year, but not enough to please the fans.

Meanwhile, Jeremy Williams was learning his craft the only way it's ultimately possible: on the field. Free safety is a demanding position for a true freshman, particularly in a complex and aggressive defense such as the one Joe Lee Dunn was then pioneering.

The free safety covers the middle third of the field—between the two sets of hash marks—and he plays both the run and the pass, depending on what transpires at the line. He must be smart, diagnosing a play quickly as the ball is snapped. He might drop into pass coverage on one play, pick up a running back out of the backfield on the next, or even blitz (go after the quarterback) on the play after that. He has to play with intelligent fanaticism, as a ball hawk with a brain.

Despite his size, Jeremy quickly earned the players' respect. They balked a little, however, at his tendency to give advice. Here was this snot-nosed kid, months off his senior prom, walking up to junior and senior starters and giving them suggestions to improve their play. Who did he think he was? Jeremy was not arrogant in any way; he showed deference to his elders. But if he saw something that could and should be improved, he didn't hesitate to stick in his nose and point it out.

The first few times he tried it, of course, there was some grumbling. But his teammates had to admit that when he spoke up, he was nearly always right. He knew how to help them step up their games in specific situations, and he did it with humility. So they found themselves listening to the pint-sized, wet-behind-the-ears kid from some place down in Georgia. And as the months and seasons went by, his leadership only became more entrenched.

He even earned a nickname: *The Georgia Assassin*. It sounded funny when you caught a glimpse of him standing next to some six-foot-five, three-hundred-pound noseguard. But when Jeremy Williams hit, he didn't hit like a little guy. He was merciless; he brought the pain. And his intensity was proven by the number of times he was knocked unconscious in games and practices. There were at least three of these, as Brett Whiddon recalls.

Jeremy Williams gave it all he had. He believed in politeness outside the gridiron, unrelenting terror inside it. He was indeed the Georgia Assassin. And no matter how tall you were, you just had to look up to him.

6

HIGH-IMPACT FAITH

SOMETIMES BRETT WHIDDON HAD TO REMIND HIMSELF that Jeremy Williams the player was the same human being as Jeremy Williams the student.

It was a kind of Jekyll and Hyde thing. On the field, Jeremy was hard-nosed, violent, relentless, and spirited, always shouting instructions or encouragement. Off the field, he was laid-back, polite, and likable. Particularly given his size, he didn't come across as the typical college jock.

Then there were the phone calls. Nearly every night, at a certain time, Jeremy was going to be in his dorm room, waiting for the telephone to ring, so he could talk to his hometown honey. The other guys were living their campus lives to the full—going to class, practice, study hall, meals, and of course out to parties. But Jeremy had to have his "Jennifer time," and he was unmercifully kidded about it. Not that any of the razzing bothered him in the least. He got so excited over those calls and letters.

These were dorm rooms, of course, with almost no privacy. Jeremy would curl up against the wall, on his bed, and talk for an hour or more. His friends wondered what in the world they could find to *talk* about for so long—and why Jeremy insisted on clinging to his high school sweetheart.

"Plenty of great-looking women right here under your nose," some teammate would say. And there were plenty of women who let him know they were interested. Most of the other guys were dating around, taking full advantage of a campus fully stocked with knockout coeds. But Jeremy was resolute. His girl was no less his girl for being eight hours away.

Some of his friends marveled at his stance. Four years stretched ahead like an eternity for an eighteen-year-old, and there was no chance Jennifer would come to Memphis State; she just couldn't afford it. Where did Jeremy's personal determination and discipline come from?

It was easy to answer that question if you caught a glimpse of Jeremy holding the phone in one hand and his Bible in another. He and Jennifer would read the Good Book on their own each day, then discuss what they'd read over the phone. That definitely made an impression on Jeremy's teammates.

It also made an impression on a couple of phone bills, unfortunately. After the first month, the couple ran up more than five hundred dollars in long-distance charges. (This was before the era of cell phones and roaming plans.)

"Okay," Kathy Bolles said when she got over the shock, "here's what we'll do. We'll find the cheapest long distance rates, and you'll have to be responsible for paying the bill."

Jennifer and Jeremy agreed. To them, it was worth it.

In between phone calls, practices, and games, Jeremy threw himself into developing his newfound faith. He was active in Fellowship of Christian Athletes (FCA). He also prayed each day, read his Bible, and listened to Christian music in the locker room and before games. He didn't believe in being as aggressive with his faith as he was with a tackle; he tried to make his witness a matter of action rather than words. But everyone knew that Jeremy Williams was serious about following Christ.

While playing football at Memphis State, he heard Steve Largent, an NFL Hall of Famer and US Congressman, speak at chapel before the Tulsa game. Largent told about his experience representing Christ in both football and government, and he made a statement that Jeremy never forgot.

"You may be the only Bible some people will ever read," Largent said. "Think about that as you move through your life each day. The people you know may never pick up the book, but they pick up on *you*. *You* are their Bible." Jeremy claimed that thought as a kind of creed.

One example was the issue of obscene language. Football fields are generally no place for tender ears; coaches and players alike typically feature colorful terminology in their vocabularies. But Jeremy had made a resolution and was going to live by it: he wasn't going to curse. His no-cuss policy became somewhat legendary on the team. Even after hard hits in the games, he maintained his Sunday school tongue.

"That guy, with the hits he takes!" someone would say. "Sooner or later, he *has* to cuss. He can't hold it all in forever, can he? You just watch. When he cusses, it'll be an event, and I want to be there."

Then one day there came the play everyone knew was coming. It happened during the Tulsa game. A massive lineman hit Jeremy full force after the whistle had blown. It just about knocked the sheer *country* out of Jeremy. The field fell quiet. Players gathered around to watch the free safety pick himself up off the ground and perhaps release the foulest string of maledictions ever heard in Memphis.

Sure enough, Jeremy leaped up, got in the face mask of the lineman who hit him, and pointed at him. His face was beet red, and you could almost see the smoke coming out his ears.

"You're . . ." he sputtered. "You're . . . *stupid!*"

The Memphis players dissolved into laughter. Even the Tulsa lineman began chortling. If that was the coarsest language Jeremy was capable of, then they might as well give up—he passed the inspection. He wasn't going to cuss. He wasn't going to compromise. He wasn't going to chase women. He wasn't going to do anything but be the person he had set out to be—a devoted follower of Christ.

ONE FOR THE AGES

It wasn't difficult to be excited about the season of 1991, when Jeremy was a sophomore. Everyone on the team was pumped for the opening game.

It was scheduled for Los Angeles. The opponent was the University of Southern California, and the game would be played in the Los Angeles Memorial Coliseum, home to Super Bowls and World Series and the 1984 Olympic Games.

Chuck Stobart, MSU's head coach, had previously been on staff at USC, so he had contacted his friends in LA to set the matchup between the two schools. But was this a wise move? Memphis State was a struggling program, and USC was among the elite.

The USC Trojans had finished the previous season twentieth-ranked and, coming into 1991, the team was sixteenth. The game was scheduled for Labor Day. It would be the first college foot-ball game of the season, with no other televised games across the country. The whole country would be watching the game on national TV.

Jeremy loved a good challenge, and so did his teammates. They knew they had been given a once-in-a-lifetime opportunity to measure themselves against some of the nation's most highly recruited players on a big stage. Most people were expecting an easy win for the celebrated Trojans. But the Tigers had a full off-season to prepare themselves for sixty minutes of regulation play to create a memory that could become their legacy. They'd taken full advantage of that, with extra hours in the weight room and full concentration when training began for the season.

Beyond matters of football, a free trip to Los Angeles was no small perk. The Memphis State team flew across the nation, then climbed onto tour buses and took in the sights of Hollywood. Memphis State wasn't in the habit of attending postseason bowls, but this trip had a bowl feel to it.

When the actual game began, it was time to tend to business. Only a tiny contingent of Memphis fans was able to attend, but everyone back home—including Columbus, Georgia—was watching. At kickoff, the team was ready to go to battle.

Though USC dominated the statistics in the first half, Joe Lee Dunn's defense hung tough, giving up only one touchdown. Jeremy made a remarkable tackle for a Trojan loss. On the play, the Trojan quarterback ran an option around the left side with a trailing running back. Jeremy's responsibility was to cover the quarterback and force a pitch. He did that. But after the ball was tossed, he came right through the quarterback and hit the running back for a loss. He had singlehandedly blown up both sides of an option play, which generally requires two disciplined defenders to handle.

Memphis State managed to tie the game at 10–10 by the end

of the third quarter, and the Tigers were beginning to see what was possible. USC was wilting a bit down the stretch, but the Tigers were well conditioned. Why not go ahead and win?

Something amazing happened then. At the beginning of the fourth quarter, Memphis State scored two touchdowns within one minute, twelve seconds of playing time. After the first of those, giving the Tigers the lead, Southern Cal mishandled the kickoff. The returner allowed the ball to bounce in front of him, and a Tiger grabbed it to set up the second touchdown. Suddenly unheralded Memphis State, seventeen-point under-dogs, had a two-touchdown lead—and the defense was pitching a second-half shutout. The final score was 24–10, an eye-open-ing beginning to the 1991 season of American football.

Coach Stobart picked Jeremy Williams as his defensive player of the game. A TV camera caught Jeremy in the locker room, describing how it felt to claim such an amazing victory: "It's an answered prayer. I'm so excited I've been crying."

On the "Chuck Stobart Show," the head coach talked about motivation. He had heard that USC hadn't even bothered to show Memphis State as its opening opponent on the schedule board. As far as they were concerned, the real opener was against Penn State. Coach Stobart had no idea if this story was actually true, but he'd used it to challenge his team—and obviously, it had worked.[1]

The downside to such an incredible opening was that the season had nowhere to go but down for Memphis State. The team that had upset nationally ranked USC on the road would win only four more games that year, though, as usual, much of the reason for this was a killer schedule filled with powerful teams from a higher tier.

Jeremy's junior and senior seasons were both 6–5 experiences, yet there were nice moments along the way. During the 1993 season, Memphis State was headed to Starkville, Mississippi, to take on Mississippi State, yet another SEC rival. The Bulldogs' head coach, Jackie Sherrill, had obviously scouted the Tigers' roster. "No five-ten, 170-pound safety is going to stop our offense," he told a reporter the week of the game.[2] Everyone was telling Jeremy about it—something like waving a red flag in front of a bull (if a rather undersized bull).

Again, Jeremy rose to the challenge. Memphis State pulled an upset, and Jeremy was the defensive MVP once more. Afterward, Coach Sherrill apologized for calling the player out. He was a seasoned, experienced football figure who had once been the national coach of the year. He had groomed Dan Marino, coached elite squads, and attended major bowls. But on that day he'd been schooled by a five-ten, 170-pound safety he hadn't seen fit to recruit.

MORE THAN A GAME

It would have been nice to have played on a championship team. But for Jeremy, college football was about something more than the win-loss record. Just sharing a locker room with a group of fellow warriors meant a lot to him.

He got to suit up with quality players such as Isaac Bruce, who would go on to a great NFL career with the Rams, and quarterback Steve Matthews, who would also play in the NFL. Larry Porter, a fine running back from Columbus who had played for Columbus High, was also a teammate. Years later, when Jeremy returned to the Memphis State campus to hand out an award in his own name, Porter would be the head coach.

Jeremy loved playing in huge pigskin cathedrals such as the Los Angeles Memorial Coliseum, Florida State's Doak Campbell Stadium, or the University of Tennessee's Neyland Stadium, where he played before 91,000 fans. He also loved helping the MSU defense become a nationally recognized force. During Jeremy's junior year, Memphis State was ranked number three in the nation on defense. Jeremy was the second-leading tackler on the team, behind Danton Barto, a future Butkus Award nominee.

But most of all, Jeremy loved having the opportunity to play out his faith as he played out his football, whether in victory or in defeat. Jeremy saw football as a way to put his beliefs into action, to show how a Christian can behave with integrity. He had many opportunities to let the message of the gospel shine through his actions.

For example, there was a game against Arkansas State during Jeremy's junior year that seemed to be a fairly routine and easy victory. The Tigers ultimately won 37–7. But an incident during the fourth quarter became the talk of college football that day.

Tiger receiver John Bush caught a pass and was tackled. But as he lay on the ground, an Arkansas State defensive lineman walked up, lifted his foot, and stomped on Bush hard enough that Bush had to be helped off the field later. By that time, chaos had overcome the game.

The stomping took place near the Memphis State sideline. It was visible enough to instigate a huge brawl within seconds. Players from both sidelines ran onto the field. Helmets were wielded as clubs. One player grabbed a metal cup holder and began brandishing it as a weapon. Brett Whiddon actually saw a player leap up and perform some kind of martial arts kick. The whole thing played out on ESPN SportsCenter later that night.

It took the coaches and referees quite a while to regain control because as soon as one fight calmed down, another one would have been sparked a few feet away. Arkansas State players were angry about the rout. MSU players were angry about the stomping.

Groups of large, athletic, and *angry* football players can quickly become powerful and frightening mobs. But Jeremy refused to be sucked into the rising flames. Instead, he did what he could to keep teammates calm. He pulled his friends back toward the sidelines, shouting for them to stay out of the fracas. As a team leader, a voice of reason, he commanded respect.

At the end of the game, when time came for the traditional midfield handshake, officials and coaches were still trying to keep the teams separated due to fear of another brawl. But Jeremy began walking toward the Arkansas State sideline. He immediately heard the voices of the officials and coaches shouting at him: "Get back on your side! Turn around, 19!" But Jeremy kept walking until he reached Ray Perkins, the head coach.

Perkins had been the head coach at Alabama. He had coached in the NFL. Jeremy thought he deserved respect, so he reached out and shook his hand. He did it because he believed it was the right thing to do. He also hoped he could visit for a moment with an old teammate from Kendrick, Delray Stephens, who played for Arkansas State. Jeremy's action was one little ray of light during a dark moment on the gridiron.

The next season, 1993, would be Jeremy's final one as a player. During that senior season, he played in a tough contest in Little Rock against Danny Ford's Arkansas Razorbacks. Undertaken in a driving rain, the game was messy and hard-played. Memphis State had been struggling that season, losing two straight and giving up 54 points to Louisville. But that day against Arkansas, Memphis brought one of its greatest defensive performances. The final score was 6–0 Tigers, the only shutout of Jeremy's years in Memphis.

None of that meant as much to him as what happened after the final whistle blew. The Fellowship of Christian Athletes contingent from MSU came to the middle of the field for a prayer huddle. A few Tiger players had been doing this since Jeremy's freshman year. The huddle had grown gradually over the years, from postgame to postgame. But this time the prayer warriors looked up to see the entire Memphis State team joining them—plus a number of Arkansas players. For the first time since Jeremy came to Memphis, the entire squad was united in prayer after a contest, locking arms with their opponent. Three hours of physical ferocity were forgotten, and suddenly it was a field of wet, tired, but friendly young men, united in faith, seeking God together.

The fans, gathering their belongings and preparing to leave, suddenly fell silent as they saw what was happening down on the field. Razorback followers were sullen and disappointed over a frustrating loss, but the grimaces now melted off many of the faces. Having been emotionally consumed by a boys' game, they were now reminded of what meant the most in life and where victory could be found even in the midst of smaller defeats.

It was one of those moments of perspective. No one who was there ever forgot it.

For Jeremy, that quiet incident summed up everything he loved about his college experience. This was his senior year, the end of the road for his football ambitions. He wasn't going to play NFL defense at his size, no matter how great his heart was.

But he was still going to be a man.

He was still going to follow Christ.

And he still planned on surrounding himself with young men like these—young men who needed a living, walking Bible among them, in case they didn't get around to reading the printed one.

Playing football was over for Jeremy Williams, but as far as he was concerned, all of that was just the pregame ceremony. The real game, which wasn't a game at all, lay just ahead. His career was set to begin, and he knew in his heart that God had special plans for it.

7

LOVE, PERIOD

LOVE IS PATIENT.

Jennifer knew that was what the Bible said. "Love is patient, love is kind" (1 Cor. 13:4). That was the modern translation anyway.

But the dusty, old-school King James Version, the Bible her parents and grandparents had once used, actually said that love "suffereth long." Somehow that seemed a more accurate description of Jennifer's experience.

Patient? That meant waiting for a dental appointment.

Suffering long? That was your boyfriend's truck pulling out onto the highway again and knowing you wouldn't see him for weeks and weeks. *Suffering long* was living that way for three long years of your young life.

It wasn't that Jennifer was angry or resentful. She was of no mind to complain. She believed with her whole heart that this arrangement was God's plan for them. And nothing in the world could have changed her mind about Jeremy. She'd rather love that man from half a world away than any man within arm's reach. Location was a real-estate factor, not a true-love factor.

All this was true, but it was still difficult to be patient sometimes.

That first trip to Memphis to drop Jeremy off wasn't so bad. Jennifer knew she'd see him again in six weeks, at the first home game, and the two of them had just enjoyed their summer together. She'd even given up an opportunity to go to Washington, DC, and vacation with a favorite aunt. Any other time, she would have jumped at the chance to travel with her family to the capital, ride horses with her aunt, see the sights, and have fun. But she had chosen to stay home, board with her grandfather, and spend time with Jeremy—their only full summer together as a couple.

That fall, while Jeremy was at Memphis, Jennifer began taking classes at Chattahoochee Valley Community College (CVCC) across the river in Phenix City. She had accepted a scholarship there and was thinking about becoming a teacher. She also worked at a horse farm that backed up to her parents' property. Jennifer found a great deal of comfort in the quiet, dignified beauty of horses. In a sense, they'd been her first love.

Jennifer used the modest earnings from her farmwork to help finance her and Jeremy's long-distance phone bills, which ran about three hundred dollars per month, and cover traveling expenses to Memphis home games. The Williams delegation made the long trips up to Memphis six times per year, when the Tigers made their Liberty Bowl home appearances.

Still, the separation was hard. Sometimes Jennifer had to lean on that verse from 1 Corinthians and remember to be patient when Jeremy would tell her about what he was doing. He'd call from California, where the team traveled to play Southern Cal, and say, "Guess where we spent the day? Disneyland!" Or he would talk about his experiences on the relatively glamorous and fun-filled campus in Memphis and then ask, "How was your day?"

She could only reply that she'd taken a test, cared for the horses, and maybe changed the oil in her car.

Jeremy was living the adventure, and she was living the life of everyday repetition. But there was no way she could hold any of that against him. It was obvious that he missed her every bit as much as she missed him. He was clearly delighted every night that he heard her voice. Their separation wasn't Jeremy's fault. It wasn't anyone's fault. It was just the price of love.

One Sunday afternoon in 1993, after he'd been home visiting, she kissed him good-bye, clung to him for a few minutes, and then stood and watched his truck disappear over the horizon. It would be the last time she had to do this. But knowing that didn't help. She could no longer bear the separation, the waiting, the dependence upon phone lines.

At that moment, overwhelmed with loneliness, Jennifer did what she always did: she sought the comfort of her horses. She found some mundane task to perform in the barn and got busy. But that was no good either. She could no longer be stoic and strong, so she collapsed against the barn wall and the hay floor and began weeping.

Somehow her father found her there. John Bolles, quiet and strong as an oak, simply held his daughter, letting her cry it out for twenty minutes. He told her that thirty days after he married her mother, he'd left for navy boot camp. After ninety days there he'd returned home for nine months, only to leave again for Guam on Christmas Day.

"The separation made our love grow stronger," he said. "And your separation from Jeremy will make your love grow stronger."

Jeremy and Jennifer had a pet phrase they shared: "I love you, period." It summed up their commitment to a devotion that had no conditions, no strings—a love that just *was*, because it came from God.

Some people, they knew, love *if*. After the *if* come the conditions, the strings attached. *I will love you if you do this for me. I will love you if you always please me.*

If that can be called love at all, it's a love that depends on something else, a love that insists upon convenience.

Others love *because*. *I love you because of your looks. I love you because of your money.* Same thing. Conditional love, Jeremy and Jennifer knew, always puts *me* first. It's a contract, an agreement that can be breached and broken at any time.

Unconditional love—I love you, *period*—is selfless. There is no *if*, no *because*, no whys or wherefores. It is a self-sustaining love, a commitment engraved in the heart. It's a love that is set on eternity, because God is eternal. It's a love that we serve, not a love that demands service.

That's the love that Jennifer and Jeremy aspired to, the love that defined what they had. And she understood that the tough things about her relationship ultimately pointed to the special things about it. Let others have easy and convenient relationships. Let them have the fast food; she and Jeremy would hold out for a banquet. In life, you reap what you sow. Jennifer and Jeremy wanted to sow a 1 Corinthians 13 relationship.

Love "suffereth long"? Perhaps. But as the passage goes on to say, it also "always protects, always trusts, always hopes, always perseveres." And most of all, it "never fails" (vv. 7–8).

Yes, that was it! Jennifer clung to those words, and the more difficult their separation became, the stronger their faith became in each other—love tempered by fire. They *protected* what they had. They *trusted, hoped,* and *persevered* toward the time when the two of them could be together for always.

Steadily but surely, the together time was coming.

Popping the Question

The marriage proposal is a venerable American tradition. Sometimes it comes as a total surprise—the question actually *pops*! It leaps out in the early, headlong rush of romance.

Other times, the relationship is a challenge, something that must be fought for. It is so serious, so hard-won, that a proposal is little more than a formality. It's no more surprising than the sun coming up that morning. Almost from the beginning, the couple has known that marriage is their destiny. It's not an *if* but a *when* and a *how.*

The first time Jeremy and Jennifer talked on the phone, back in that momentous summer of 1989, they talked for two full hours. It was as if they'd known each other all their lives. On the first date, it mattered not a bit that the movie was a poor choice; their personal connection was at the wow-plus level. Long before the first trip to take Jeremy to Memphis, the two of them knew their paths would intertwine into a single, endless highway to diverge no more.

So the proposal, which came at the midway point of Jeremy's college career (halftime, in football terms), was not much of a surprise. His first two years were finished, and two more remained. It was time to talk about a future together, and they both knew it. The question was: when and how would the question be popped?

Jennifer made one thing clear. "Jeremy," she said, "don't you dare make me wait on some expensive diamond ring! I don't care a thing about that. Just get me any old cubic zirconium thing, and I'll be happy. Or just give me the pop-top from a Coke can—okay, maybe not that. *Don't* give me a pop-top! I just don't want you to think I have to have a diamond. What matters to me is that it's *you* putting the ring on my finger."

Jeremy grinned, "Well, you're getting a nice hunk of stone whether you like it or not, so get used to it."

And he was as good as his word, working an entire summer to pay for the ring he had chosen for his girl. They worked together at the farm, where he cut the grass under the hot sun as she cared for the animals. This would be a big moment, proposing marriage. It's one of those times when a man realizes he must do it right. Jeremy would not take the cheap or easy route—or the predictable one.

Once the ring was in hand, it all came down to the Question. It was definitely going to happen that summer, but when?

Jennifer thought she had it figured out. There was a big family reunion coming up—the perfect time for Jeremy to clear his throat, tap a spoon on a glass, ask for everyone's attention, then make the big announcement. He'd pop the question, she would dissolve in tears as she said yes, then everyone would applaud and gather 'round to fawn over the ring.

Okay, maybe that was dreaming. Jeremy wouldn't want to do this thing in front of a bunch of people. Maybe he'd propose to her *before* the gathering. Then she could just show up at the event, flash her hand, and let the fawning begin.

She began to drop little hints. "Did I mention that thing coming up, Jeremy? That thing with your whole family?"

"Nineteen or twenty times, yeah."

"Well, I just don't want you to forget. Remember, people will be looking at my left hand. They'll be nudging you and putting you on the spot."

"Okay, I've got it covered," he nodded with a coy smile. That's how he continued to play it—before the gathering, during it, and after, when he *still* hadn't proposed.

What was going on? Jennifer was perplexed. The reunion had been the perfect venue, and he'd missed it! She was on pins and needles for a week, and she knew her impatience was high comedy for Jeremy. She couldn't say a thing about it, of course. That was the beauty of it for him. Popping the question was the elephant in the room, and it would be discussed only when Jeremy decided it was time.

When the moment did arrive, it came out of nowhere—or that's the way it seemed to Jennifer. They were out by the swimming pool at the Bolles home, and Jennifer was sitting in the "love swing." Her father had built the swing for his and Kathy's anniversary, actually carving the words *Love Swing* into the frame. So in a way, it was the perfect place for question popping after all.

Except that Jeremy, down on one knee, kept complaining. "This is really uncomfortable," he said. "Why do you have to have this gravel surface?" His knee was grinding right into the pebbles as he showed her the ring and delivered his carefully rehearsed proposal.

Jennifer was laughing as she said yes. There was a hug, a kiss, and then she hit him on the head and berated him for not giving her the ring earlier. "I'm so mad at you!" she growled. "I wanted that ring to show off at your family reunion!"

Her tears of joy, however, suggested that she wasn't angry at all. So did the fact that she was holding on to him and wouldn't let go.

Jeremy just grinned and let his fiancée hang on as long as she wanted.

Tying the Knot

By Christmas they had decided to get married the following summer. The plan had always been to wait until after graduation, but they couldn't be patient any longer, and their parents understood.

John and Kathy Bolles gave their consent, but on one firm condition: Jennifer had to finish college when she could. They knew how easy it would be to become so consumed by wedding planning, then moving to Memphis and beginning a marriage, that she would never quite get around to getting that degree.

But Jennifer had no intentions of falling short of her goals. She had finished the two-year program at the community college in Phenix City and was about to begin the rest of her college degree closer to home, at Columbus State University. By next summer she would only be three courses and a student-teaching requirement short. Then, after the couple came back from Memphis, she could complete her degree at Columbus State.

After another long year of separation, the wedding finally took place on June 19, 1993. The venue was the Bolles place on County Line Road, way out in the country.

Jennifer's family home was set at the end of a long driveway, and they had a pool, a barn, a fishing pond, and a pasture back behind the house. There was plenty of room for a festive outdoor wedding—just the thing for this particular couple. John had built a gazebo by the pond, but for the ceremony he moved it to a position overlooking the pasture. It made for a beautiful setting.

Everything in the world that Jennifer loved was a part of this day: Jeremy, her family, her friends, her horses, and her God. The family pastor, David Howle from Edgewood Baptist Church, emphasized covenant and commitment in his charge to the bride and groom. Marriage, he said, is a holy covenant between a man, a woman, and their Lord. Jesus is first and foremost in a marriage, the one who has brought the couple together, the one they serve together, the one who binds them together as one flesh.

Jeremy was delighted with everything about the day, but particularly the opportunity to bring together the best of his Memphis family with his Columbus family. Several of his teammates had driven all night to be present, and Jeremy had asked an old buddy from the neighborhood, Larry Margarum, to stand with him as his best man. Larry, who had moved to Wisconsin, was touched by the honor. He loved Jeremy and wouldn't have missed that day for the world.

After the ceremony, everyone enjoyed a picnic meal of Southern-fried chicken, potato salad, baked beans, coleslaw, and a wedding cake specially baked by Jeremy's Aunt Angie. Jennifer and Jeremy toasted each other in champagne glasses etched with their names and the date, but filled with Dr Pepper rather than bubbly. The photographer admitted that this was a first in his wedding career.

Then, at the end of the day, the bride and the groom did the fairy-tale thing. They mounted Jennifer's pair of horses and galloped off into the sunset. Riding away with her knight in shining armor (if not helmet and shoulder pads) had always been Jennifer's dream. Now it was actually happening. And as everyone she loved in the world stood together to watch and applaud, she had to admit it had been worth every moment of the wait.

MARRIED IN MEMPHIS

After a short honeymoon on the beach in Panama City, Florida, Jeremy had to report for football camp in Memphis. He still had his senior season and one more year of school to get through. Jeremy was, as always, an outstanding student. In 1995 he would even earn a Hitachi/CFA scholar-athlete award worth five thousand dollars for postgraduate study.

The couple happily moved into student housing, though finances would continue to be tight. They used Jeremy's $345 monthly food allotment for paying the rent, then ate as cheaply as they could.

To bring in a little more money, the new Mrs. Williams worked at two different veterinary clinics.

In the first of these clinics, the only opportunity was as a receptionist—nothing in the way of working with animals. But the second position gave her the opportunity to do a little of everything. She cleaned teeth, anesthetized animals, and helped put down pets that were beyond medicine.

Jeremy, by then, had gotten most of his tough academic requirements out of the way, so he was living the casual, fun-filled life of the senior who has taken care of business. One day Jennifer came home to find him out in an adjoining green area driving golf balls. *Typical Jeremy,* she thought. *He's got to find some game he can play, some place to compete.*

She parked the car, walked out to see him, and they shared a warm kiss—still newlyweds. But Jennifer looked at all the golf balls and couldn't figure out the point of the exercise. "Baby," she said, "what are you aiming at?"

Jeremy pointed to a signboard at medium distance. While

she'd been watching, he hadn't hit anything close to it. He drove another one, and it was wide right by thirty yards.

"You're not Joe Allison," she said. Allison was Jeremy's team-mate, an All-American placekicker.

Jeremy hit another, and another. Wide right every single time.

He grunted and teed up the last couple of golf balls. "Save me one," Jennifer said. He looked at her with faint amusement. She had no history as a golfer.

He tossed her his club and a ball, stood back, and folded his arms as if to say, "Show me."

Swoooosh. Jennifer followed through. The ball rose in a tall arc, then came down, bounced once, and hit the sign—*pop!*

Jennifer screamed and jumped up, brandishing the golf club over her head in a victory pose. Her husband rolled his eyes. "Beginner's luck," he said. "You couldn't do that again in a million years."

"Throw me that last one."

He did.

This time, Jennifer's drive traveled in a laser shot toward the sign, where it rolled between the two supporting posts. Bull's-eye.

"Whoooooooo!" Jennifer performed another victory dance as Jeremy quietly collected his clubs and began walking back toward the car. He was murmuring something about "new clubs." It was *their* fault.

By and large—golf notwithstanding—it was a perfect first year. On Fridays of game weeks, Jeremy still became the property of the football team. He would ride with them to stay in a hotel—standard college football practice to keep the players together and focused. But the rest of the time, he belonged to Jennifer and she to him. Like so many newlyweds, they were short on cash and long on dreams. The future was a vast, blue and cloudless sky, and only God knew the plans he had for them.

They had passed the test of three years' separation. Now, whatever came, they would face it together. They would face it emboldened by the love God had given them—a love that "always protects, always trusts, always hopes, always perseveres."

That truly "never fails."

The dark clouds would come; they always do. The couple couldn't begin to imagine the tests that lay in wait far down the road. But they believed in their hearts that God had strengthened them, prepared them for some great and eternal purpose—and that when the time came, his grace would be sufficient for whatever that purpose might require. For not only did they love each other, they also loved their God.

Period.

8

THE GOOD LIFE

JENNIFER SET DOWN A BOX OF FOLDED CLOTHING AND paused to wipe her sweaty brow. "So," she said to her husband, "how many boys and how many girls?"

"What? You're still on that?" Jeremy laughed. "Okay, let's see. I'll say nine boys and seven girls. We can herd them all in the pasture with your horses."

Jennifer scowled at her husband. "Be serious."

"I really don't know, honey. I haven't given it a whole lot of thought. The way I look at it, whatever God sends us will be a blessing, right?"

"Of course! But I like thinking about our future. You think it's best to have a boy first, or a girl?"

Jeremy said, "Honey, you like to map everything out, don't you?"

Jennifer stood her ground. "I like to know where I'm going. Don't you?"

"Absolutely. I've always been pretty organized. But I also take things as they come a little more than you do. Like they say, life is something that happens while you're making other plans."

Jennifer thought for a moment. "What's the Bible's version of that? 'A man makes his plans, but the Lord directs his course.' Or something like that."

"Hey, direct my course with this box, will you?" said Jeremy. "Which room?"

Jennifer rolled her eyes in mock indignation and pointed him toward the laundry room. "It's not that I'm really in a hurry to start a family," she said. "I think we should wait awhile."

"Well, like I've said, I'm happy whenever God sends a baby. I'm ready tomorrow."

"No way. This time is for us to baby each other. Let's enjoy being just the two of us while we can—get our roots put down, you know? And then there will be time for babies."

"Time for nine boys, seven girls?"

"You're hopeless. You know that, don't you?"

The two of them were carrying their things into the Bolles residence, the site of their wedding. Not that there was all that much to carry. After a year of marriage in Memphis, they possessed little other than each other. And like most newlyweds, they felt all the richer for it.

It was July of 1994 and the plan, which they'd concocted together, was for them to live with Jennifer's parents for a while. There was plenty of room, and they were welcome there. "You're just starting out," Kathy Bolles had said when she invited them, "and your dad and I want to give you the chance to save some money for a down payment on a house."

Staying with the Bolleses would also allow the couple to wait for just the right house to become available. It needed to be somewhere not too far away, with a good school system for the future babies. Pastureland was a must for the two horses Jennifer had owned since she was twelve. And, of course, the house needed to be affordable on one income, since an important component of the plan was for Jennifer to stay home with the children they would have.

It would take a little time to save up earnest money and find a home matching those specific needs. Neither of them were the impulsive type; they wanted to lay a strong, sure family foundation. And they had a few matters to take care of in the meantime.

Jennifer still lacked those three courses for her college degree, which she would eventually earn from Columbus State with magna cum laude honors. She also needed to meet her student-teaching requirements, and she wanted to go back to work at the farm. Jeremy was already telling her she didn't need to work, but Jennifer wanted to put away money for that home. She had always dreamed of a shining knight and a castle, she said. Now all she needed was the castle.

But even more than that, her husband needed a job.

Jeremy was focused on joining the workforce as a high school football coach. From the time he was a freshman at Memphis State, giving advice to seniors on the team, it had grown increasingly obvious that coaching was his destiny. His own coaches had told him, "Williams, you're a good communicator, and a leader of men. You have a sharp football mind. You need to be doing what we're doing."

Jeremy could see what they meant. Coaching definitely fit into his gift set. It played to his passion for athletics, his competitive spirit. But above these things, he thought in terms of serving God. On the field, he played for God's glory. How could he best serve God's kingdom now that he had graduated with a bachelor of science in education degree, with a major in health and physical education? The coaching profession would give him an excellent platform for working with young people and living out his faith as a witness to them.

Every year, he would have a squad of young men—kids at the crossroads of life, trying to find their way. He'd been there himself only five or six years earlier. A football coach had an extraordinary opportunity to be a mentor, a second father, or even a surrogate father at times. In today's world, he knew, there are increasing numbers of kids who don't have fathers in their homes.

Manchester High School, forty-five minutes from Columbus, looked promising. The school was rebooting its football program. The head coach was retiring. Assistant Greg Oglesby was being promoted to take his place, and a staff position was opening up.

Jeremy had considered staying closer to Columbus, where he'd have easily found a position. He knew the schools a little better in his hometown, and the shorter commute would have been nice. But he also saw the wisdom of making a fresh start somewhere new, somewhere he wouldn't be the hometown kid. Manchester was a perennial power, a team that often advanced through the play-offs. The facilities and support were very strong.

So Jeremy interviewed to be an assistant football coach at Manchester High School. Coach Oglesby didn't know him personally, and neither did Zeke Geer, his defensive coordinator. But they were aware that Jeremy had grown up in Columbus and played for Buzz Busby, a hard-nosed, well-respected football coach. They knew Jeremy had started four years at safety in Division I NCAA football. He came across as intelligent, polite, and eager. Very strong credentials.

Jeremy got the job, and his coaching career began.

NEW KID IN TOWN

At the ripe age of twenty-two, Jeremy was a rookie in his profession. A visitor to practice might have mistaken him for one of the players. But he didn't behave like a timid newcomer. The other coaches quickly noticed that he radiated self-confidence and a sense of direction. He knew his football, he had a strong work ethic, and he wanted to help mold a team of champions. So Coaches Oglesby and Geer didn't see him as a young protégé to be molded and taught. They felt comfortable treating him as a colleague. He was ready.

The coaches had seen their share of blue-chip athletes in their time, players born with all the skills. Some of them had gone on to star in college, and a few of those had come back to coach high school ball with the air of conquering heroes. But once they donned the cap and whistle of the coach, they were out of their element. They couldn't rely on physical talent anymore, and they were lost.

Jeremy Williams had none of that false bravado about him, no "this is how we did it in college" arrogance. He adapted to his new environment very neatly. But he did have the advantage of still being in playing condition for the most part, his body chiseled by four years of NCAA-level strength training and conditioning. He could still run something close to a 4.4 forty— forty yards in 4.4 seconds. These abilities definitely gave Jeremy an edge with his kids. Athletes can "sniff out" other athletes. The players were in awe of a coach who could outlift and outrun nearly anyone on the roster.

Defensive coordinator Zeke Geer took to Jeremy right away. Zeke was a certified country boy, a free spirit who sowed seeds of laughter everywhere he went. He had a keen appreciation for the Western novels of Louis L'Amour and a tendency to speak in cowboy lingo, and he spray painted a pair of shoes silver and wore them on game days. In Jeremy he welcomed another all-around guy who wasn't above a little foolishness. "Jeremy is one you can ride the river with," he told Coach Oglesby. "He's one of us."

So Jeremy had a smooth transition with both players and peers. Just about the only thing he didn't like about his position was being assigned to the booth during games. The booth is the area at the top of the stadium where public-address announcers, statisticians, officials, and a coach or two sit. The booth coach takes advantage of what he can see from this height. He uses a headset and talks to his colleagues (and sometimes the players) over a communications system. The input is invaluable. But to Jeremy, being up there was like being in exile.

"Feels like I'm not even at the game," said Jeremy. "Most of the fans are closer to the action than I am. C'mon, Zeke, you take the booth this season."

"You know we can't do that," said Zeke. "Coach O wants you up there. But it's not because you're low man on the totem pole or being punished or anything like that. The way we look at it, it's an honor to be up there. I depend on you to tell me how the other offense is setting up, because I can't see a dang thing from the sidelines."

"Yeah, but you can talk to the players as they come off. You can slap the guys' pads, get in their grills, and fire 'em up. *That's* coaching—not sitting up in the clouds with a walkie-talkie."

Jeremy complained, but he understood there were dues to be paid. His time would come. Someday he would be a coordinator like Zeke, then have his own program like Coach Oglesby. Then he could do all the pad slapping and grill shouting he wanted.

ON THE ROAD AGAIN

It was well known that Jeremy Williams never cussed, never drank, never smoked, never lied. But Zeke Geer soon learned you had to put an asterisk next to that last one. Jeremy wouldn't lie *unless* he was pulling a prank on somebody. If he had a good one going, he'd play the part, and he might tell you any crazy thing to keep you going. In the middle of whatever it was, Zeke would say, "Jeremy, tell me the truth now. Do you swear you're telling me the truth?"

An innocent look would come across Jeremy's face, and he would say, "Zeke, you know I don't swear." And that's all you'd get out of him. When it came to jokes, he might bend the truth here and there, but he could always stand behind the safety of his no-swearing policy.

In important matters, of course, Jeremy's word was his bond, and he did his best to live with integrity, even in tough moments. His peers noticed that he was no different on business trips, when others might be tempted to relax their standards and let off a little steam. The coaches regularly traveled to Atlanta for clinics and recertification. After a day of seminars, many of them would convene at the local tavern.

Zeke would look around and see a number of coaching colleagues who were overindulging in the booze, and he had to wonder about the hangovers he'd see at the next morning's early sessions. But Jeremy, the dedicated teetotaler, would be right in the middle of them, laughing and clowning around. He'd be nursing his soft drink and having just as much fun. Living his beliefs didn't mean being a stick-in-the-mud around his coworkers.

The coaches had meager traveling expenses for these trips,

so they pinched pennies. Four of them would take a room with two doubles, with two coaches sharing each bed—quite a snorefest. Jeremy and Zeke tended to be bunkmates. Zeke, the older man, took a little longer to get to sleep, and he noticed how often the two of them turned over at exactly the same time. He'd turn on his right side, and Jeremy would turn on his own right side. He'd roll onto his back, and Jeremy would follow suit. It looked choreographed. Zeke said it was like "synchronized swimming," and the two of them joked about it for years.

Zeke also claimed that one night he felt a strange, ticklish sensation on his bald head. He opened his eyes to find Jeremy fast asleep but smiling slightly as he patted the top of his defensive coordinator's head. "Jeremy, wake up!" he snapped. "I'm not Jennifer! I'm not Jennifer!"

But that was just who Jeremy was: the kind of guy who was at home with anyone in any setting.

WHERE THE HEART IS

Jennifer wasn't sleeping quite so well. Why hadn't anyone warned her that teaching required superhuman abilities?

After getting her degree, she began teaching science at Manchester High, where her husband was coaching. She taught biology, ecology, and human anatomy, as well as college preparatory courses.

It was fun to have the same workplace as Jeremy, almost as if the two of them were making up for those years of being so far apart. Teaching, however, had proved quite an adjustment for Jennifer. She had always been a good student, and teaching ran in her family. But she'd had no idea how hard a job it can be.

When you teach, you're on your feet all day, fighting to educate rooms full of teenagers who'd rather be anywhere else. You go home and put in several hours preparing for the next day. Then you go to bed, you get up, and you do it again. There were stacks and stacks of papers to grade. Then there was discipline to maintain, paperwork required by the state, and several different class preparations to cover.

Jennifer leaned not only on her husband but particularly on her mother during this time. Kathy, who knew her way around a classroom, kept her from discouragement and reassured her that it was all going to get easier.

At least there were the school holidays and the opportunities to spend time together as a couple—though Jeremy was busy during much of the summer, preparing for football. The couple knew things would be different when they had children, so they tried to take full advantage of this season of life. They enjoyed a cruise to the Cayman Islands, and one Christmas they visited the Florida Keys. On weekends, Jeremy indulged his passion for hunting, while Jennifer attended horse shows. It was a good period of their lives, and time began to accelerate, as it sometimes does for those who are moving joyfully through it.

Then one day they got a call from Monica Evans, their real estate agent. Whenever that happened, Jeremy and Jennifer paid close attention, because they only heard from Monica when she'd come across a house with real possibilities. "Drop what you're doing and come see this place," she said. "It's just right for you."

The house was in Pine Mountain Valley, not far from Franklin D. Roosevelt State Park and FDR's "Little White House" at Warm Springs. The three-term president loved this area of Georgia, where he came for treatment of his paralyzed lower body. He built a home there, and visited often during the later years of his life. He called it his "Garden of Eden" and could often be seen driving through the Harris County countryside in his hand-operated car. He was in residence at the Little White House when he died in 1945.

Because of his affection for the area, Roosevelt made sure his famous New Deal plan for the country included projects to help local residents of the area get back on their feet after the Great Depression. The Pine Mountain Valley Resettlement Project, begun in 1934, was part of that effort. It was a kind of social and agricultural experiment that involved relocating impoverished farmers and sharecroppers and helping them build homes with land to farm. New concepts in crop management were part of the plan. If the project went well, its techniques were to be used all over the United States. Unfortunately, the plan was abandoned in the early forties, as programs were cut in favor of the war effort. But 210 homestead units—"valley homes"—were completed, and Pine Mountain Valley still has a few descendants of the original farmers who took possession.

Jeremy and Jennifer were shown a remodeled valley home, a modernized relic of the era. At first sight, Jeremy eyed the property with skepticism. "There's not enough pasture for your horses," he protested to Jennifer.

"Babe, just come look at the house!" Jennifer said. And when Jeremy stepped through the door, he knew this was just what the two of them had been looking for. There were three bedrooms, stenciled walls, a cozy fireplace. A family room had been enlarged by removing a wall.

Jeremy and Jennifer offered earnest money that very day and moved in during February 1997. Now they had their little house in the country with seven acres and two horses.

There was work to be done, however. Those horses needed a barn. For months Jennifer's dad, Jeremy, and Jennifer spent their Saturdays carrying lumber, hammering nails, and roofing. Jennifer's mother, brother, and uncle lent an occasional hand and various tools.

But there was a notable absence: Jeremy's father had passed away suddenly in March 1997, just a month after his son and daughter-in-law moved into their new home. He had visited the house twice and loved it.

Jeremy, who had adored and revered his dad, grieved through the spring and summer. He'd been ready to start his adult life, but not to lose such an irreplaceable part of his earlier life. It helped a little to work on these Saturdays, to pound away at those planks of wood, to level the dirt floor and put in the fence—simply to stay busy. And he felt a bittersweet pang as his thoughts turned to the grandchildren he had hoped to put in the lap of John Williams.

It's a Girl

Children. More and more, Jeremy was feeling their absence.

For several years he and Jennifer had been the cute young couple on the faculty and at church. They'd enjoyed the freedom to travel, to take off and pursue their passions. But now felt like the time to start filling the nest they had established.

Jennifer, the planner, had thought in terms of teaching five years, giving birth to a beautiful child on cue, and then, fourteen to fifteen months later, bearing child number two.

But time, like one of her horses, had moved from a trot to a gallop. It was 2000. Jeremy was now a defensive coordinator and weight-room coordinator at nearby Harris County High School, and he would be thirty years old the following year. In football terms, it was getting close to halftime, and it was time to put some points on the board.

"So Jennifer," he asked her one day with a smile. "What about the plans?"

"Plans?"

"You had it all mapped out. But I've looked all over the house and I can't find those two children we were going to have by now."

Jennifer laughed. "I know, I know. It's time, isn't it? I'm as ready as you are. I guess life happened while we were making other plans."

"But God is still directing our course."

A few months later, a positive home pregnancy test, along with a doctor's confirmation, showed that a baby was on the way. But the couple kept their secret for three months. They wanted to get through the common period of miscarriages before going public with the news everyone was eager to hear.

In early 2001, Jennifer invited her parents, along with Jeremy's mother and sister, to dinner. After the meal they sat together over hot chocolate and chatted. Then Jennifer brought out a package for everyone to unwrap. Inside was a tiny baby bib.

No more explanation was needed—everyone was hugging, laughing, and crying.

Josie was born July 4, 2001, a lovely and healthy baby girl who looked like her mother and, as time went on, shared her mother's best traits. Jeremy was over the moon with the joy of being a dad. Jennifer, as per the plan, retired from teaching to stay home and care for the infant.

Life was kind to the Williamses during the late 1990s and

early 2000s. Jeremy and Jennifer often sat outdoors with Josie, watched a Harris County, Georgia, sunset, and thought about God's rich and abundant blessings. Jeremy still had career goals, but he was happy in his work. He still looked as if he could suit up and play defense with the best of them. Jennifer was enthralled with the adventure of motherhood. Josie was doing something new and wonderful every day.

This is what contentment feels like, they thought. Maybe FDR was right. Maybe Harris County really was the Garden of Eden.

They savored the glory of the moment, never suspecting the tests that awaited them just over the horizon.

9

STEPPING UP

JEREMY WILLIAMS PAUSED TO LOOK ACROSS THE EMPTY football field. A quiet, rural landscape cradled Leon Coverson Stadium on three sides. He savored the moment of calm before the storm.

Soon it would be time to climb on the bus and lead his young men into battle. Jeremy felt the quickening of heart and mind that always ushered in game day. It was about the sound of cleats on a locker room floor, the troops clustering near the exit, the snaps of several dozen chin straps to helmets. It was bands playing, parents shouting, the smell of popcorn from the concession stand.

Oh, how he loved these moments, these rituals.

It was August 30, 2002—opening day for high school football season—and Jeremy Williams's debut as a high school head football coach. How many nights had he laid awake imagining what this would feel like?

It felt good.

Some would have noticed that the sky was overcast, that the home-field grass was a little bald near the big G on the fifty-yard stripe. Jeremy saw nothing but blue skies, green grass, and open-field tackles yet to come. He had no time for glass-half-empty attitudes.

Jeremy Williams was thirty years old, in the prime of life, and in perfect health. He was married to his high school sweetheart, Jennifer, who had given him his beautiful one-year-old daughter named Josie. They lived in a cozy home in the quiet pastures of Pine Mountain Valley, in the heart of Georgia.

Until now his life had lacked only one thing, and that was a football team to call his own. Now, here in Greenville, he had that too.

For good measure, he had brought along two of his best friends to help him coach these players—Chip Medders and Tanner Glisson. The three of them were determined to make the Greenville Patriots the new football power from Meriwether County, and they'd come prepared to offer their supreme effort toward that goal.

Now, after a sweltering, shouting, whistle-blowing summer of getting acquainted with the players, it was showtime.

Jeremy checked his watch. Time to get moving. He needed to change into his coaching gear and glance at the game plan one more time. Then he would get the boys on the bus, get them focused and ready to hit. The game was in Zebulon, where Greenville would be opening against the Pike County Pirates.

Jeremy opened a door, saw his two assistants, and chuckled.

Chip and Tanner were changing their shirts in a glorified utility shed. That image seemed to capture the whole experience of coming to Greenville.

At Jeremy's previous two schools, field houses and decent coaches' quarters could be taken for granted. He and his fellow coaches had nice desks, file cabinets, blackboards, and places to keep their stuff. But what Greenville had to offer was a dank storage room they shared with a dusty lawnmower, a few old tools, and some broken furniture. It wasn't exactly a "war room" for the gridiron brain trust. It reeked of gasoline, and the floors were greased with motor oil.

This was Greenville. This was their mission.

Chip looked up as he tucked in his shirt. He said, "Hey, Jeremy—what the heck have we gotten ourselves into?"

And that got them laughing again, all three of them. Positive and ambitious as Jeremy was, it had been evident for several weeks that the mountain they had elected to climb had a very steep face.

The three friends had their work cut out for them.

THE ROAD TO GREENVILLE

Their friendship had been built just down the road in Manchester, a town that had a strong, positive identity. When you crossed the city limits, the sign informed you that you were entering the "City of Champions."

Local folks embraced that image. Manchester had four times the population of Greenville, though Greenville was the county seat. The cotton mills had moved in a few decades back, and the resulting jobs meant homes and families. Only four miles away was Warm Springs and Franklin Roosevelt's home away from home—a major tourist attraction. Callaway Gardens, one of the state's favorite showplaces, was also nearby. And Manchester could boast of being the hometown of Stuart Woods, a *New York Times* best-selling author. Manchester residents were proud of

their town, and they made sure their high school fielded a con-
tender nearly every season.

During Jeremy's first season as an assistant coach in
Manchester, the Blue Devils played for the Class-A state championship. In his fourth year, in 1997, his team won it all—a coveted
state championship. As an intense competitor who craved winning, Jeremy had chosen a good spot.

He made enduring friendships at Manchester as well,
including the one with his defensive coordinator, Zeke Geer.
Jeremy also really hit it off with another young coach on staff,
Dennis "Chip" Medders. Their wives bonded quickly as well.
Jennifer Williams was a science teacher; Ava Medders was a
special-education instructor. The men shared a love of hunting,
particularly for deer and turkey—and, of course, they lived and
breathed football.

Jeremy, Jennifer, Chip, and Ava were a tight unit. Hardly
a Saturday night went by that the two couples didn't take in a
movie or at least share dinner. As high school coaches, the men
knew their career paths could lead them in separate directions at
any time. But there was an understanding that they'd do everything possible to keep their careers interlocked.

In Manchester, Jeremy coached defensive backs. One of his
star pupils in the early years was a high-energy athlete named
Tanner Glisson. Years later, after Tanner finished college and
Jeremy became the head coach at Greenville High, he would give
Tanner a job on his staff.

Jeremy's career was on the fast track to success. As an assistant under Greg Oglesby at Manchester for five years, he was a
quick study. Then, in 1999, Harris County's coach snapped him
up as a defensive and weight-room coordinator. But after a few
years at Harris, he began to sense that God wanted him to step

out on faith and enlarge his horizons. Was this time to make his move into the head-coaching realm?

Jeremy and Jennifer were people of prayer, and he wanted to get it right. So he prayed and waited for some sign from heaven. Just about that time, two head-coach positions in the area came open. One was right in front of him, at Harris County High School, where the head coach had moved on. Naturally Jeremy wanted this one. He wouldn't need to move, because he was already in place, and he knew both the kids and the program.

The other opening was in the town of Greenville, twenty-five miles to the north. If Harris County had been a renovation project, Greenville was a tear-it-down-and-build-it-back situation. The Patriots had won state championships twenty years earlier, but those glory days were long past. Greenville offered a much higher risk, but potentially higher rewards.

Jeremy and Jennifer asked God to make his will known in the interview process, and Jeremy discussed the situation with his friend Chip Medders, who was still over at Manchester. Chip was feeling the same pull within him, the urge to move on. He just didn't think of it in the same spiritual terms—though, as always, he was fascinated by the way Jeremy talked about his faith.

Jeremy wasn't overly pious. He didn't throw around spiritual lingo in every conversation. Yet you could see his quiet confidence in the ways and the will of God. He believed in the kind of God you didn't just talk about, but talked *with*—a God you could take with you when Sunday church was over and who would show you the perfect plan for your future.

Chip, who had also grown up in the Bible Belt, considered himself a Christian, but not at such a depth of seriousness. As he told his wife, "Jeremy walks a higher path. He's not fooling around when he talks about God. That's his whole *life*."

Others knew all the holy talk, but too often they turned out to be fakes. Not Jeremy. Chip admired the way his friend carried himself, and he wondered: Would the day come when he, Chip, would find himself on that higher path?

Double-Teaming Mr. Josey

The two men were on the phone together, plotting and planning like two bank robbers devising a heist.

"Well," said Chip, "I did it, Jeremy. I went ahead and put in my name for Greenville, right next to yours. So may the best man win. You've got a little more experience, but I've got my own connections, remember? The principal who's interviewing us—Mr. Josey? He was my old shop teacher here at Manchester when I was a teenager myself. And I know all kinds of people in Greenville."

"Problem is, they know *you*," kidded Jeremy. "But listen, man, I hope you get it. You at Greenville, me at Harris County— that would be sweet. Can't you see us on separate sidelines, trying to outcoach each other?"

"Oh *yeah*," said Chip. Then he paused for a minute before saying, "Or maybe we're on the same side. Maybe we'll go somewhere together, like we always talked about."

"I'd love it. Chip, you know I would hire you in a heartbeat."

"Same here."

So the seed was planted. When Jeremy was not offered the job at Harris County, that seed took root. Missing out on his first choice was a disappointment, though. Not making the cut was hard on someone with Jeremy's competitive nature.

But Jennifer offered comforting perspective. "Don't worry

about it," she said. "When God closes an opportunity, that only makes your decision a little easier. Now you know a place he *doesn't* have in mind for you."

"Well, *I* had it mind for me," Jeremy answered.

"It just means there's something special in store for you in Greenville. Or if that doesn't work out, we'll just have to cast our net a little wider."

"Yeah, who knows? Maybe over into Alabama."

There had never been a year when somebody somewhere didn't need a good football coach. They knew God would work it out. He always did.

As Chip Medders knotted his necktie and headed for his interview with Mr. Josey, his onetime shop teacher, he knew that his best friend would be coming in on the following day. Chip had decided to put in a good word for Jeremy.

He sold himself first, describing what he had to offer as a football coach. Then he said, "Let me tell you a little bit about the guy who will be sitting in this chair tomorrow—Jeremy Williams. He happens to be my best friend, and he's one of the finest men I've ever known. He's good with the Xs and Os, and he's good with kids and relationships. He's a family man, and in general I'd say he's an outstanding coach and an even better human being. Whoever hires him is going to hit a home run."

Mr. Josey was impressed. He'd never interviewed anyone who campaigned on behalf of his rival for the job.

Chip paused and slyly added, "Now, the way I look at it, you can get Jeremy Williams in one of two ways. You can hire me as your head coach, and I know for a fact Jeremy will come along as part of the package. Or you can hire *him* for the job, and he's going to hire me. Why settle for just one of your best candidates, right?"

The next day, Jeremy's interview went very well. Chip's phone rang not long after that. It was Mr. Josey. "Hey, Chip," he said. "I've got some good news and some bad news for you. The bad news is that you didn't get the head coaching job. The good news is that we want you to come in and work with Coach Williams, just the way you spelled it out."

"It's an honor," said Chip. He smiled, thinking about the way Jeremy had described praying about his future, his confidence that God would work things out.

Jeremy and God, Chip observed, seemed to have a pretty good thing going.

A Mountain to Climb

Jeremy Williams and Chip Medders were set to take charge of the Greenville Patriots—and Tanner made three. Tanner Glisson looked up to both men, who had coached him in Manchester days, and when offered an assistant's job he quickly signed up for what promised to be an exciting ride. The three of them got together early in 2002, dreamed their dreams, and began preparing for their debut season.

Before the two weeks of spring practice began they visited Greenville High and met with their future players in the cafeteria. Jeremy and Chip had state championship rings, and they had made a point of wearing them for this first meeting. They flashed their rings around prominently as they sold the dream of returning championship seasons to Greenville.

"Y'all have got yourselves a tough coaching staff, and we want you to know that," said Jeremy. "We're going to do things the right way, and the right way is the way *we* show you to do it.

Anybody planning to test us on that won't be on the team long. But we think you're ready to win some games. Anybody in this room ready for some wins?"

A few kids said, "Yes, sir."

"Anybody tired of the other schools coming in here and hanging forty or fifty points on you?"

Again, there was a muted response.

Jeremy said, "So you men have a great couple of weeks before spring practice begins. Try to stay in shape and work out as much as you can. Be ready to bust your tails when late April rolls around."

The kids clapped politely. They seemed to be good kids. But Chip and Tanner exchanged glances as they saw the Greenville football culture firsthand.

The raw material was there. Manchester had played Greenville in football, and there had seemed to be some good athletes, maybe Division I college-potential athletes. But up close, you could see that these players were soft. There was a lot more fat than muscle in evidence. And you couldn't look across the group and pick out a first-player-off-the-bus guy—that kid you put at the head of the line to make an intimidating first impression on your opponent.

One problem was the lack of weight training. Jeremy was a firm believer in a football program fully equipped with organized strength and conditioning; it was the physical foundation of any team. These players had no muscles, no fitness, which meant they'd be knocked backward on every play.

Another problem was the football players' lack of discipline. The previous coach, John Maynard, was a likeable fellow who simply didn't have a mean bone in his body. He loved working with the kids, but he didn't want to be the head man anymore. He'd remained on staff and fit in well, but it just wasn't in him to shout and threaten and go ballistic. Jeremy, Chip, and Tanner had a great fondness for him, and they kidded him about his "excess niceness." But now, they believed, it was time for some excess toughness.

The whole program, in fact, needed an upgrade. Though Manchester was just fifteen miles down the Roosevelt Highway, it felt like a world or two away. The field was in awful shape, the stadium hadn't been renovated since at least the 1970s, and there was no field house at all. The program gave off an aura of neglect.

Jeremy knew that you can't win without first establishing the will to win. It was all about the way kids saw themselves. And it wasn't just a football thing—the whole school needed an attitude adjustment. As he walked through the halls of the school, he found himself breaking up fights or going into classrooms to pull out students who couldn't be controlled by the teachers. The student-body attitude wasn't a positive one. School spirit was no more than a distant rumor.

"We only thought we were signing up to turn a football team around," Jeremy told Chip and Tanner. "Turns out we signed up for a whole school. The team is just a symptom of the bigger problems."

Chip said, "I think you're right. We came here for football, but it's bigger than that. We need to be there for Greenville High, not just for the Patriots."

Jeremy went to the principal and told him that he was going to need some things—most of all, support from the school administration. In exchange, he said, "We're going to do things that will lift up the whole school. We're going to get all these kids motivated and show them what it means to have pride in your campus."

Mr. Josey quickly agreed to help. "You come and tell me what you need, Coach," he said. "Up to the limits of our budget—and those limits are pretty severe, you know—we'll do everything we can to get you what you need."

Jeremy told Chip and Tanner, "Guys, I said it to the players, now I'm saying the same thing to you—get ready to bust your tails. We've got us a mountain to climb. These kids don't have the first idea what it's going to take to win. And job one is getting them into the weight room. If we're going to build up this program, we'll have to build up some bodies."

His first request was for the school to put in a weight-lifting class. The idea was to have all the players enroll and let the coaches teach it, pushing them hard each day. It was going to be an eye-opener for most of the kids, who were strangers to disciplined work in the weight room.

The coaches converted an old PE classroom in the back of the gym. Chip's dad personally built the benches and squat racks. The various weights were brought in and a training cycle was established.

From then on, it would just be a matter of getting the kids to push themselves.

DARING TO DISCIPLINE

Other problems cropped up as spring practice got underway. For one thing, Jeremy was shocked by the players' casual approach toward football. They treated it like some ordinary after-school club.

Jeremy had played his high school football in Columbus, where Friday night lights were a given in the community. The schools there were talent factories, and recruiters from Auburn, Georgia, Alabama, and other major college powers were frequent visitors. Jeremy had quickly learned he would never see the field without maximizing his abilities. He lacked size, so he'd had to outwork everyone around him just to get his shot. For him, that had meant hitting the other guy so hard that the coaches couldn't help but notice.

Then, in college at Memphis—the only school that offered a scholarship to an undersized tackler—he'd had to fight his way onto the field again. Soon enough, they were calling him the "Georgia Assassin," and he was almost legendary as a heavy hitter who sacrificed his full body down after down until the whistle blew, until the clock expired. The Memphis coaches only wished they had a few more undersized assassins.

In coaching, he'd been with Manchester teams that went 14–1, 13–1, 10–2, and 14–2. The last of those won the state championship game by three touchdowns. After an 8–3 1998 season, he had gone to Harris County, a team that had never been to the play-offs, and helped take them there the second season. Harris County had never beaten Manchester before, but that happened while Jeremy was on staff.

Taking practice casually, in other words, was a concept Jeremy Williams could not grasp. He and his assistants were accustomed to success, but it was clear they weren't going to get it until the players started to take the program seriously. They didn't push themselves. Their fundamentals—blocking, tackling, footwork, ball protection—were terrible. Worst of all, players regularly showed up late for spring practice. Their lackadaisical attitudes drove all three of the coaches crazy. They would shout at the players, make them run, and threaten them, but nothing would change. As a matter of fact, when the coaches "got in their grills" and hollered, the players might actually talk back. What kind of team culture was that?

It was clear that the players didn't understand what it took to have a winning football program. Trying to explain it was ineffective. There would have to be a tipping point, a crisis moment when something happened that drove the point home—the point being *discipline*. When that moment came, Jeremy would have to recognize it, and he would have to exploit it to the fullest.

There were two offensive linemen who were late for spring practice more frequently than anyone else. They were upcoming seniors, they were experienced, and they were essential to any chance of winning. Of course, they realized that. The way they had it figured, they were so irreplaceable that they were above any laws the coaches laid down. They'd come trotting down the field twenty minutes late, day after day. They flaunted their lateness, smirking. The rest of the team would watch the spectacle. Then they'd look over at the coaches and see them steaming.

Something had to give.

Chip and Tanner were privately politicking for Jeremy to drop the hammer. But he wasn't certain. It wasn't that he valued winning above discipline. He just tended to err on the side of believing in people. Surely he could get to these two linemen, make them see the light. Then the rest of the team wouldn't have to suffer.

"I don't think that's going to work," said Tanner. "They're making fun of the whole system, out in the open. And everyone's watching."

"I agree with Tanner," Chip said. "You've got to take control, or we'll lose them all. Make an example of these guys."

Jeremy sighed as he thought about it. Being late for practice had never been an option on any of his teams as a player or as a coach. Maybe his two friends were right.

With spring practice over, Jeremy reflected all summer on

the advice of his assistant coaches. Late in the summer, Jeremy told Chip and Tanner, "Okay—if they're late on the first day of fall practice, the hammer comes down."

Chip and Tanner nodded gravely.

"Matter of fact," Jeremy said, "I'll make it into a dang spectacle. But we've all got to agree—no turning back once we do this. If we back down at any point, we'll ruin the lesson and make discipline into a joke."

"Agreed," said Tanner.

Still, on that first day of fall practice, it was impossible not to wonder if this was a huge mistake.

Here came the two seniors, trotting casually down the hill, twenty minutes late for no particular reason. Chip and Tanner spotted them and began hurling the obscenities. Jeremy, of course, *never* cussed. But he made up for it in sheer volume. He went full-scale Armageddon on the two boys. His face turned red as he began shouting at them, berating them, charging right up to their face masks and giving them both barrels of his windpipes.

"So you guys think you can make your own rules?" he roared. "Not on this field! Not on my team, by gosh!"

He pointed a finger back up the hill. "If you don't want to play *my* way, then get up that hill and don't come back!"

Time seemed to stop; birds seemed to fall silent. The last echo of Jeremy's voice bounced across the adjoining farmland, and the sun hid behind a cloud.

All the players stared with wide eyes. The whistles slipped from the other two coaches' mouths, and they almost dropped their practice schedules.

The two late players hesitated as if they weren't sure they'd heard right. But Jeremy held his ground. Hands on hips, he stared fire at the two seniors until they turned and slowly walked back up the hill.

Practiced resumed. And this time, when the coaches said, "Hustle," the players hustled. The practice suddenly became crisp, determined, and yes, *disciplined*.

It was a turning point in the history of Greenville football.

10

STANDING FIRM

AND SO IT CAME: THE AFTERNOON BEFORE THE SEASON
opener against Pike County, over in Zebulon.

Jeremy had paused to look over the stadium. He had dressed
in a utility shed with his two friends, chuckling over the sheer
indignity of the thing. Now it was time to climb onto the bus.

Jeremy stood next to the driver's seat and addressed his players. "You guys ready?" he said.

"Yes, sir!" the players shouted.

He offered a few words to fire them up—standard head
coach stuff. Then he told them to think over the game plan,
review their assignments, and get ready to buckle 'em up and
play four quarters of tough football.

As he sat down, Tanner whispered to him, "We could sure
use two senior linemen."

"And who was it who told me to put the hammer down?"
Jeremy whispered back.

"Just saying, this is one of the few games on the schedule we
might have any chance to win."

At Manchester, Pike County had frequently been served up as a homecoming game—one of those schools people expected to beat. The game was indeed winnable, *and* it carried the extra urgency of being the opening game. For these reasons, tonight represented a must-win opportunity for Greenville.

But on the first play from scrimmage, the Pike running back broke free and ran eighty yards for a touchdown while the Greenville defense stood, hands on hips, and watched. They looked as if they had no clue how to make a tackle. Weeks of instruction in practice seemed to have missed the trip.

Chip was up in the press box on the headset, slamming down his notebook, filling the airwaves with choice language—to no avail. Greenville lost that game 25–19. As the whipped team filed back onto the bus, Tanner sat down right behind Jeremy and whispered into his ear, "We just went 0–10."

Jeremy didn't have much use for negative talk, but he knew Tanner might not be far from the truth. Losing to Pike County was a rough way to launch a new season and a new job.

The next game, Greenville's home opener, ended with a dismal 34–0 loss to Jackson High, followed by a 21–0 loss the next week to Callaway High. More and more, Jeremy pictured those unthinkable numbers: *0–10.* How long would an off-season seem after that?

The coaches weren't taking it well, this new "league doormat" experience. Jeremy found himself working hard to keep them from giving in to discouragement. Deep down, of course, he had enough frustration for the lot of them. But he had to lead, to keep the attitude aggressively positive. "By gosh, every place you go, there's problems," he would say. "We just got to keep coaching 'em up. No reason we can't get it turned around."

"Yeah, but what gets me is the ones who look like they don't care," said Chip. "Sometimes it's all I can do not to grab 'em and shake 'em. Good thing it's not Tanner or me in your shoes, or we'd be kicking kids off this team right and left."

Jeremy thought about that. "The thing is, it's easier to kick them off than to change them, isn't it?"

Point taken.

THE BOND

Jeremy preached this message to his coaches over and over: change is a process. If you wanted to make it all the way to the top, you had to do some heavy climbing. There weren't any ski lifts to the top of that particular slope. To get up there required patience, persistence, and a refusal to look down.

In Greenville terms, that meant taking the kids they had and sticking with them.

"We've just got to coach our tails off," Jeremy kept saying. "We're here to change people, not chase them."

So they redoubled their efforts. They pushed and prodded the players and applied a level of discipline the kids had never experienced.

But it wasn't all gritted teeth and threats. Off the field, the key was relationship building, which required more time and focus than coaching.

They saw the kids every day in the weight room, where they built toughness, shouted encouragement, celebrated new lifting records. They saw them in the halls of the school, and in the lunchroom. There was a new grade requirement for playing football, and if the players didn't meet it, they had to stay after practice for special help; so the coaches made themselves available to tutor the kids who struggled with their studies.

Then, of course, there was football practice in the hot Southern sun. After that, it was time to get the kids home.

The Greenville players lived all over the area—up and down highways, across country roads made of nothing but Georgia clay, along every byway in Meriwether County. When practice was over, Jeremy, Chip, Tanner, and Coach Maynard headed off in different directions with their pickup trucks and minibuses packed wall to wall with big, sweaty kids. On those rides, coaches became big brothers, mentors, and friends. There was laughter, talk about life outside football, team bonding.

One day Tanner dropped off a freshman wide receiver, a truly talented athlete who would end up playing college basketball. "I'd like to step inside and say hi to your folks," Tanner said as he pulled up at the small home.

They walked up, and the player pushed the door open. "Watch your step—seriously," he said. Tanner saw that the floor was nothing but dirt, and there was a massive hole that had to be avoided as he stepped in.

After the years in Manchester, this was eye-opening stuff. "These kids—for too many of 'em, we're all they've got," said Tanner the next day as he told the story to Jeremy.

"That's why it's going to take all *we've* got if we're going to make any kind of impact on their lives," Jeremy said.

Chip and Tanner couldn't help but wonder if even that would be enough.

Reason to Believe

Big Deon was five-foot-six, three hundred fifty pounds of unathletic clumsiness. He lacked even more in the way of self-esteem. His eyes said that he saw himself going nowhere in life—an African-American kid in a small Southern town, no money, no prospects. If he managed to pass all his courses and end up with a high school diploma, that might be the highest accomplishment he could hope for in life. At least that was the story his eyes told: *I'm not much. Don't waste your time on me.*

It was one of many similar stories that caught Jeremy's attention. He simply wasn't going to let kids like that be beaten down and have their whole lives dictated by their surroundings. Somehow, he and his staff were going to show Deon and the others that life had its blue skies, its open fields—that if they believed in themselves, worked hard, and worked together as a team, life could open itself up in remarkable and powerful ways, no matter who they were or where they came from.

Jeremy believed strongly that God wanted joy and fulfillment for every child in his family.

But how could he make *them* see that?

It was a little embarrassing now to think about how brash, how ambitious, they had been when they first arrived in Greenville, flashing those championship rings. They had been naïve, but there are far greater sins. The point was that here they were, this was the task they had taken on, and they were going to lift this team and this school up or go down trying.

But where to start? Everywhere they turned was some seemingly impossible task—whether it was teaching Big Deon to block or getting a decently groomed football field that didn't announce to one and all that "losers play on these weeds."

Chip was the one who took care of that shaggy, weed-infested football field. When he got sick of looking at it, he bought a lawnmower himself and began cutting the grass. That's what it took at Greenville. If you saw a need, you didn't put in a request. You did whatever you could to fill the need yourself.

Before long, entire families were getting into the act. Chip's sister bought Powerade for the players at halftime every week. Chip's dad built the benches for the weight room. The wives did whatever they could, including being phenomenally patient with their absent or discouraged husbands.

Sometimes it was the little stuff that made a big difference. The coaches saw there were no team traditions, for example. How could this be? Traditions created lifelong memories and pulled a band of brothers together. So the coaches would have to *invent* some traditions. At Manchester, the team had eaten steak for its pregame meal every week. At Greenville that wasn't going to happen, so the team started getting together for a Hardee's double bacon cheeseburger. The players thought that was living pretty large. The Hardee's gatherings made game nights feel a little more special.

Living Color

Meanwhile, racial realities had to be allowed for. The team was 90 percent African American. The coaches were conscious of being three white dudes, Manchester's "fortunate sons," riding in on their white horses to put their stamp on a mostly black culture. If they weren't careful, they could be considered condescending and paternalistic.

Jeremy intended to balance his staff racially once the season was over. But for 2002, the three white dudes would have to make it work. Only sincere caring would bridge any gap of distrust. It was like parenting, really—time and love have no substitutes. Teaching Greenville to believe would have to go deeper than just driving the players home. The coaches had to be themselves, let it all hang out a little.

So they did, more so than they had with past teams. They let their more playful side come out on road trips, in school, on the drive home, or whenever they had a chance. They used fun and laughter to disperse the tension. That might mean wrestling on the floor with Big Deon, the "round mound of fourth down," until everyone was laughing and shouting. It might mean sitting around and shooting the breeze, not letting on that they were tired and would rather be home with their families. It might mean brushing up on algebra so they could tutor the defensive tackle who was struggling with that subject.

It definitely meant taking off their shirts in thirty-five-degree weather and climbing into a fall-festival dunking booth as students and parents whistled and jeered at them in delight. Years later, Chip would remember coming close to backing out of the frigid dunking. (Was this thing worth a bad chest cold?)

But they'd come too far to back down. Tanner kept thinking about the house with the hole in the floor, the kids with holes in their lives.

Once he and Chip had said that if it were up to them, they'd be kicking kids off the team right and left. They weren't thinking such things as often anymore. They were beginning to see what Jeremy could see. They were knocking themselves out, but it was worth it. Love never sits on a fence. It jumps in—even if it's into a dunking tank in November.

One more time, at the fall festival, Tanner said, "Hey, Chip— what have we gotten ourselves into?"

Then the two of them laughed, exchanged a high-five, and threw off their shirts as they took turns climbing into the booth of frigid water.

11

BREAKING THROUGH

EVERY TOWN HAS A FEW FAMILY NAMES THAT ARE ingrained in community life. One of those names in Greenville was Bray. The family had produced a steady flow of fine athletes, and Kevin Bray was no exception.

Jeremy knew what an exceptional football player looked like. The coach had played against Alabama and Tennessee. He'd been to Los Angeles and suited up against Southern Cal in the stadium where the Rose Bowl is played. And he recognized Kevin's talent as next-level ability. The other coaches agreed. Even if he didn't make a Division 1-A school, he could easily play 1-AA or Division II.

The problem was, Kevin couldn't see in himself what the coaches saw in him.

One afternoon Jeremy and Kevin sat down near the practice field for an in-depth talk. The discussion wandered from football to life itself. Chip and Tanner wandered up, and soon they were part of the conversation.

"I'd like to be really good, sure," Kevin said with a shrug. "I just don't have what it takes."

"Kevin, c'mon," said Jeremy. "You think you're in a better position to say that than I am? I'm your coach!"

Kevin shrugged again.

"You're a junior," Jeremy added. "You're sixteen years old, and you haven't even stopped growing yet. You haven't discovered everything your body can do."

Chip said, "You're just that close to breaking out, Kev. Believe it."

"I don't see why it's any big deal. I mean, we're 0–3. We might not even win a game this season. Sometimes I don't even know why I'm playing."

"You're playing because it's a great game," said Jeremy. "And it's a great game because it's a reflection of *life*—winning versus losing. If you can set your goals and bust out on this field, you can set your goals and bust out in whatever else you do. Football is just life played out in a helmet and cleats. Did you ever think about that?"

Kevin shrugged again.

"You're one of the best we got. There's no limit to what you can do in the next year. But it won't just happen by itself. You have to work. You have to push yourself, give us more than we're seeing."

Tanner said, "It may seem like a long way off, but this game could punch your ticket to a free college education. You've got that potential, Kevin."

"You really think so?"

"We do," said Jeremy. "But if it happens, it'll only be because you worked your tail off—starting today." He stood. "Now let's take it in. Hustle!"

Privately the coaches shared Kevin's fear that the team could go the whole season without a single win. Sometimes the frustration was unbearable. But it was important to avoid letting the players see their doubts.

Finally, the fourth game of the school year, it happened: the team won a game. Jeremy had not known a simple win could feel so good.

It came against Crawford County High School, and the Patriots celebrated in the locker room afterward. "Hey, doesn't that feel a little better than losing?" Jeremy called out.

There was a loud cheer, some fists slamming into lockers, some feet stomping the floor.

Jeremy said, "How 'bout that Patriot Pride? I say we do this again next week!"

It mattered in no way whatsoever that some of the guys had seen the game referred to as the "Toilet Bowl" on the Internet. You had to start somewhere, right?

Jeremy was still swimming in adrenalin as the coaches walked out to the parking lot, the three of them enjoying the moment. "Have you thought about this?" asked Jeremy. "We've got Tri-County next week, and they won three games last year. *Three.* Guys, we got us a chance to go for back-to-back victories—and to grab one on the road. Do you realize how we could build on that with the kids?"

"Boy, that would be something," Tanner said. "You could almost see the confidence creeping into their eyes tonight—the will to win. We need to hit this hard all week."

The whole season was looking different. Maybe the team had turned a corner, and they would make a big comeback in the second half of the season.

Then, on Monday, Kevin Bray didn't show up for practice. Unthinkable!

The coaches wanted to beat their heads against the school's brick wall again.

One step forward, three steps back.

STANDING FIRM

The law had already been laid down. Two players had been run off the team just for being late.

The problem was, Greenville was running the veer, a split-back offense that was all about the running backs. And to run the veer, they needed Kevin Bray.

Kevin hadn't done nearly enough to be kicked off the team. He wasn't a repeat offender, but the coaches couldn't look the other way, either. If they swept an infraction under the rug—especially one by the team's star—they would undermine every lesson in character the coaches were trying to teach.

After much discussion with Chip and Tanner, Jeremy decided to hold Kevin out for the first half of the Tri-County game. That would probably be enough to ruin any chance the Patriots had of grabbing their all-important second win and putting together a modest "streak." So Kevin's punishment would be everyone's punishment.

Jeremy sat down again with the junior. "You know I'm disappointed in you, don't you, Kevin?"

The running back hung his head. "Yes I do, Coach."

"Do you realize how much pressure I'm under to pretend this never happened and play you anyway? You know how tempted I am just on my own?"

"Yes, sir."

"I can't do it, Kevin. Winning games is very important to

me. But you know what? Competing with integrity is even more important. I care more about your character than I do about my coaching record."

Kevin looked his coach in the eye and let the words sink in. It was a lesson he would never forget, especially after listening to Coach Williams and the others puffing up his potential earlier. They thought he was all that, but they were still willing to sit him on the bench and lose because of it?

Kevin stood on the sideline during the first and second quarters of the Tri-County game and listened to angry Greenville parents and fans letting the coaches have it. What kind of coach would bench his best player just for being a kid and messing up? The team had started to show some promise. Didn't this new coach want to win?

Kevin watched how the coaches stood firm, ignored the loud criticism, and went about their work. He was furious with himself. If he'd been in the game, Greenville would have won going away. He was sure of that. Even now, his teammates were fighting for all they were worth, and he was proud of them. For the first time, he felt as if he understood what it meant to suit up as a Patriot and represent his school on the field, what it meant to be there for his team—and just how much he had let them down.

Tri-County built a 21-point lead in those first two quarters. Kevin pounded the bench with his fist as he watched it. *Hurry up and get here, second half!*

After halftime, Kevin Bray put on his helmet, charged onto the field, and the Greenville fans stood and cheered. Jeremy thought, *Did I just see that under his helmet? Did I see that gleam of anger and determination we've been trying to get out of this kid?*

Greenville launched a frantic and furious comeback, actually tying the game in the fourth quarter. But there was only so much they could do. They were fatigued, played out. The Eagles finally surged to take victory at 40–33.

"I'm sorry," Kevin was telling his teammates as they walked off the field. "This one's on me. I'm sorry!" He said those two words over and over. Jeremy was pretty sure he would not miss another practice. And he never did.

"Shake it off." Jeremy came up behind Kevin and put a hand on his shoulder pads. "Play like that next week, and by gosh, we'll get 'em!"

In the movies it might have worked out that way. But as Jeremy had said, football was life in disguise—for better and for worse.

Greenville never won another game in 2002.

The opposition was simply too strong. The Patriots lost 55–13, then 55–14 the following week—matching humiliations. There was a very close game against Manchester, of all places; Jeremy, Chip, and Tanner lost to their old head coach by only six points, 20–14. Maybe that was reasonable, but Jeremy wanted to win. So did the other coaches and the team.

The season ended with a 47–7 thrashing at the hands of Henry W. Grady High, a downtown Atlanta high school. Everyone, coaches included, was exhausted. Everyone was ready for the final seconds of the season to tick off.

They were more than a little ticked off themselves.

"The games are over," Jeremy told the team, "but you're not going to rest. I'll see every one of you in the weight room Monday except the seniors."

He watched them clean out their lockers and felt a surge of affection. But he couldn't ease up now.

"Hey, if you think we worked you hard *this* year," he said, "you better get prepared for the off-season. Because when September of 2003 rolls around, you're not going to recognize yourself in the mirror. You're going to be *chiseled*, every one of you—gonna have muscles on your muscles. We're going to out-work Grady and Manchester and Lamar County and all the rest of 'em. Right?"

"Yes, sir!" said the players together. But you could hear the weariness, the toll of the weekly routs. The kids were ready to go and just be kids for a few months.

"I wanna hear that like you mean it!"

"Yes, sir!"

"You know *when* you're going to win all those 2003 games? Before the opening kickoff. Before the band plays. You're going to win 'em during the winter, during the spring, during the summer in the weight room. While those other guys are out running around with their girlfriends, eating ice cream cones, you're going to be working your tails off, by gosh—increasing your reps, building toughness."

Jeremy turned toward the door. "I love you guys, and I'll see you Monday."

And that was it. In the blink of an eye, the 2002 season was in the books. All the planning, all the shouting, all the exhorting and the exasperation and the Xs and the Os—all of it was done.

As the last of the players left the locker room, the coaches looked at each other and heaved a collective sigh, almost in unison. "Well, what are we going to do now?" asked Jeremy.

"I think we go home and see if we still have families," Chip replied. And with one more backslap, they turned off the lights, locked up, and went their separate ways.

A Nice Spread

"Hey, you guys, look at the schedule," said Jeremy during a summer coaches' meeting. "Notice anything?"

The others just stared at the list of games.

Jeremy solved the riddle for them. "See how many times we're somebody's homecoming?" he pointed out.

The guys rolled their eyes. "I don't think that's anything new for Greenville," said Chip.

"Granted. But we'll take that challenge this year. We'll send a little message that if you schedule the Greenville Patriots for your homecoming, we're liable to spoil your party."

The others laughed—three of them now. Dell McGee was the newest member of the coaching staff. He was a sharp young African American coach from Columbus, a former teammate of Jeremy's at Kendrick High School. He had also played for an undefeated 1993 team at Auburn, started all his games as an upperclassman there, and been drafted by the NFL's Arizona Cardinals. In time, he would return to Columbus to coach at Carver High, where he would become a respected head coach in his own right.

Jeremy and his assistants were chomping at the bit for summer camp to start. Not only had they added Dell, but they had overseen the players for nearly a year now in the weight room. The players were starting to pass the sight test; some of them looked pretty good stepping off the bus.

They felt pretty good too—you could see that. Some of them were developing that elusive winning demeanor known as *swagger*. There was more confidence in practice, a stronger will to dominate the opponent. They were proud of their newly chiseled physiques and the way they had sweated off the fat. And they were as eager as their coaches to see how it all translated to football success.

Jeremy thought back to that first springtime meeting in the cafeteria, when most of these same kids, out of shape and not too interested, had clapped politely. Now they were becoming *men*. They'd pass the coaches in the hall and say, "I'm ready for it, Coach! Bring it on. I'm getting that starting job."

It was a remarkable dynamic for a team that had finished the previous season 1–9.

The coaches had made changes in their own approach too. One day during the discouraging last month of the 2002 season, they sat watching another lousy game tape on the VCR. Jeremy was sitting on an ottoman so he could be closer to the set. "By gosh!" he would bark. "Wrap up the tackle!"

Chip and Tanner sat behind him. Truthfully, they were sick of game film, weary all over, ready for the season to be put out of its misery. Chip found it excruciating to watch the kids' fumbling attempts to run an offense that did not fit nor highlight their abilities.

Chip thought about that last part.

"No!" Jeremy pounded his fists on his knees. "Lock away the dang ball!"

Chip cleared his throat and threw caution to the wind. "I'll tell you what," he said. "We need to scrap this split-back veer offense."

Tanner shot a glance at Chip as if to say, *Have you lost your mind?*

Jeremy's back was very still, but the tape paused. "We need to go to the spread," added Chip, addressing the rigid back.

Slight pause again. The shoulders tensed up. Without turning around, Jeremy snapped, "If you want to run that spread crap, you can go coach at some other school to do it!"

Chip and Tanner shared a wry grin. It wasn't out of the question that they'd take his advice. Almost anywhere they went, the job would have to be easier than this. Hey, ditch digging would be less grueling. Anything.

But they were loyal to Jeremy, just as he was loyal to the split-back veer offense that had been his bread and butter at Manchester High School.

"Just saying," said Chip. "The veer isn't engraved on Moses' tablets or anything. There are other offenses."

Jeremy grunted and resumed the tape.

And that was that—until, after the season ended, Jeremy walked into the coaches' office and said, "Men, I've made a decision. We're ditching the split-back veer and going to the spread."

"Great idea, Coach!" said Chip. He stuck up his palm, and Tanner slapped it. The three of them laughed.

The staff piled into a couple of cars and traveled over to the town of Barnesville in Lamar County. Coach Mark Wilson of Lamar County High, on his way out, was willing to hand over his whole playbook to his eager Meriwether County visitors. He showed them all the ins and outs of the spread offense. The great thing was how amazingly simple it was.

"We can sell this thing," Jeremy said on the way home, barely able to contain his adrenalin. "It's basketball on grass— we'll throw it all over the field. The kids are going to love it."

He was right. The new offense was a big hit with the players, and its implementation seemed to bring home a big message: New year. New team. No more beat downs. Or at least no more being on the wrong end of the beat downs.

Over the next few years, the spread offense would live up to its name, spreading all over the South like kudzu. It was a perfect match for high school athleticism in the Peach State.

WORST TO FIRST

The feel of summer practice was entirely different in 2003. Even learning a new offense, the players were comfortable with their coaches and ready to work. There was a focus that hadn't been there in 2002, a pride that had begun in the weight room and was manifest in hot, sweaty August combat.

Kevin Bray, the veer running back as a junior, would be the spread quarterback as a senior. It was just the kind of challenge he needed: step up, lead your team, make this new offense work. Jeremy and the others had him believing he could blossom into a special player with a little determination and work. He was looking good in the early practices.

A few hours before the opening game of the season, Jeremy stood on the top step of Coverson Stadium—the same place he'd stood a year ago. In some ways, it seemed more like a decade ago. What if he had known then what he knew now: that nine defeats, many of them humiliating, were waiting for his team in that fall of 2002?

And what about this new year? Would it live up to his hopes?

Once again, the opponent was Pike County High School. But this year it was a home game, and it would be the perfect measuring stick for Patriot progress. Greenville needed to take Pike County down. The kids needed it. The students needed it. By gosh, the coaches needed it!

Jeremy closed his eyes briefly and prayed, thanking God for letting him have this opportunity. He asked for the strength to do and say the right things—nothing that might dishonor Christ in any way or set a bad example before these young men. He prayed that God would keep the players on both teams healthy and safe. Then he looked up at the blue sky, took a deep breath, and headed in to change clothing.

Several hours later, shouting and laughter echoed in the locker room. Greenville had beaten Pike 31–14, and looked something near dominant doing it. Kevin Bray had run the offense like an all-star. The spread, still new to the kids, had proved effective. And the defense had been aggressively nasty.

The Patriots had beaten a team that finished 6–4 the previous year, but you'd have thought they'd clinched a championship. The school would be a fun place on Monday morning.

"The way I look at it, the season is three hours old," said Chip with a big grin, "and we've already matched last season's victory total."

Everyone laughed.

"Nice start," Jeremy said. "But we can be better. You ain't seen nothin' yet. We're just getting warmed up." He was hungry for bigger and better things, and he wanted to keep the team hungry.

At practice the following Monday, the coaches led a crisp, demanding practice. The players hit hard and sprinted from one drill to the next; there was no letting up until time to go home.

But once again, the streak couldn't be sustained. Greenville traveled to Jackson that Friday night and lost 42–25.

"Don't you hang your heads," shouted Jeremy afterward. "Don't even think about slipping backward. Ain't happening! Last year these guys shut you down, 34–0 in your house. And they won nine games, might win ten this season. I don't like losing either, but we're not giving in—not an inch. We've worked too hard."

The coaches pushed hard to keep the team believing, and sure enough, Greenville won its next three games. One was a road win, 54–13, over Crawford County High School. Another was a very satisfying revenge game, 66–10, over Tri-County, the team that had received the advantage of Kevin Bray's absence the year before.

Kevin was clearly determined to score enough points to make up for the lost first half. And now everyone in the region was talking about the quarterback, as both runner and passer. "He's our first success story," Jeremy told the other coaches. "But not the last." The quarterback would go on to throw for more than 2,000 yards and rush for more than 1,500—eye-popping stats from a single player—as region player of the year.

Jeremy walked up to Kevin one night after a particularly big game and said, "You believe me now? About your potential?"

Bray just grinned back. He did, as it turned out, succeed at the next level, playing football for Reedley College in California, then finishing up at Valdosta State.

MOVING ON

Once the offense got humming, it was clear how the 2003 season was going to go. And the defense was by no means shoddy!

The players enjoyed being a homecoming opponent that refused to go by the script. There was special motivation in knowing their team had been scheduled as a breather. It was fun to go on the road and crash someone's party.

In the space of one off-season, the Patriots had gone from always being the nail to often being the hammer that does the pounding. Their coaches' dedication, along with a lot of hard work from the players, had brought them here. Now, the players believed those coaches—who were friends, mentors, surrogate fathers, and drill instructors—could walk on water.

Greenville lost a tight game to Macon County, which had a suffocating defense, but took the last four regular-season games with runaway scores. In 2002 Greenville had been shut out twice and held to 7 or less two other times. In 2003 they put up 54, 66, 52, 42, and 46 points in different games. And Greenville beat their rival Manchester for the first time in the school's history.

The Patriots finally found their ceiling when play-off time came. They lost to Americus High School in the first round, and the score wasn't particularly close. But the big news was that a one-win team from 2002 had made it to the postseason in 2003. The future was promising indeed.

After the season was over, Jeremy met with Chip, Tanner, and Dell and thanked them for all their hard work. "Hey, boss, what do you think of the spread now?" asked Tanner, suppressing a grin. "Do you still think Chip and I should go to some other school to 'run that crap'?"

Jeremy fired back, "It only worked because I coached it so well."

Chip said, "Jeremy, seriously, the job you did this year is going to get your phone ringing. I guess you've proven you can coach some high school ball. Like the song says, if you can make it there, you'll make it anywhere."

Jeremy scowled. "I don't care about any of that," he said. "I'm right here until God tells me to go somewhere else. I happen to like it here."

"You sure about that? You might like going someplace with a real weight room, real facilities . . ."

Jeremy looked Chip and Tanner in the eyes for a moment, then said, "Why do I think this is leading up to something?"

His two friends shared an awkward glance.

"Jeremy, I wouldn't take anything for this experience," said Chip. "I have a state championship ring on my hand from Manchester, and this season tops that one, as far as I'm concerned."

"But?"

Tanner said, "But we have the opportunity to go to a bigger school. One where we don't have to dress in the toolshed!"

This wasn't entirely unexpected for Jeremy. It was one mark of success—people came and recruited your assistants.

Chip grew serious. "Coach, you know how we love working with you. And we'll still be best friends; ain't no changing that. You and Jennifer are family, always will be."

"Of course."

"But Tanner and I, we're just dog-tired after these two years. It's a lot of hours per day here. We just can't keep up the pace."

"I know." Jeremy nodded. "I wonder sometimes about it myself. Anyway, you guys pray about it. Go where God wants you to go. You're the best."

Chip was excited about his future. The two years at Greenville had forever changed the way he saw his vocation. But there was a part of him that felt he had more to learn from Jeremy Williams. Some voice deep inside was telling him that he had learned a lot but had missed the most important lesson of all.

And a lot of things were at stake.

Soon, he would learn what that lesson was.

12

CHIP'S STORY

It all came back to the 2002 season. Chip Medders was certain of that.

During that difficult autumn, the evil first crept into his home like a thief in the night.

So many good things had happened in Greenville, even with nine losses. The epic struggles of 2002 made the break through of 2003 possible. But there had been one bit of collateral damage.

The coaches bit back a lot of frustration that fall while the team was losing—Jeremy perhaps most of all. But he stayed the course; he was strong for everyone. If he, as the head coach, the CEO of Greenville football, let discouragement win the day, everything would fall apart. His assistants would follow his example. And the players? They'd have had one more message that they weren't good enough, that they could never be winners—one more reason not to hope for the future in football or in life.

Jeremy wasn't going to let that message set in. He fought the good fight, kept the faith, and demanded a positive, disciplined approach, no matter how high the loss tally climbed.

Chip and Tanner understood that, and they hung tough, but they sometimes got together privately to vent. They were obsessive winners like their boss, and losing was making them crazy. It was hard to face one more Friday night, one more humiliating rout at the hands of some program down the road with nicer uniforms, a better weight room, and a greener field.

Parents griped. Local papers second-guessed every move. Chip and Tanner were too competitive to take all of it lying down. They needed a forum to show they knew their football, since their team's scores seemed to say otherwise.

So the two of them began betting on football games. They bet mainly on college games with a few bets placed on NFL games.

For Chip a pattern quickly developed. Friday night would bring another frustrating loss. On Saturday, Chip would watch college football and place some bets.

It seemed pretty harmless at the time, at least the way he rationalized things. Who could deny him a little extracurricular diversion during a miserable year like this one? He wasn't betting to make money, really. It was about evaluating talent and matchups. He could even argue that this was a way to keep his football instincts sharp—study up on that game, put down a few bills, maybe salvage a small piece of satisfaction out of another lost football weekend. He would bet on several games at twenty-five or fifty bucks a pop and more or less break even—get a few right, get a few wrong, no harm, no foul.

At first.

Then, over time, came those inevitable thoughts of hitting it big. *What if I could convert three lost bets into winners each week? Or what if I put down a few more dollars?* Gambling is so seductive for this very reason: it entices with hopes that seem just within reach but never quite materialize.

Time passed. The tribulations of 2002 ended, and the triumph of 2003 followed right behind it. Chip enjoyed the validation that the turnaround brought. But by this time, it didn't matter with regard to betting. He was hooked.

Chip was happy coaching at Greenville. He felt no more need to prove anything to himself or to anyone. But those phone calls to the bookie had become a mainstay of his life—even as he and his wife, Ava, had become parents.

Someday he would quit. He knew that day would come—maybe after one really profitable football season. He'd quit, no problem.

Someday.

No Fun Anymore

One someday comes at the price of many squandered todays.

Somehow Chip's betting habit continued for nearly seven years. At Greenville, Jeremy knew it was happening, but he said nothing. It wasn't his style to tell his assistants how to run their personal lives when he was asking so much of them in the unique challenge that was the Greenville Patriots.

Still, it made Chip uncomfortable that Jeremy Williams, a man he admired so much, knew about the gambling. The two of them had been close friends for years now, but there were areas of Chip's life that he knew Jeremy would never share.

The years passed. By late 2008, Chip knew he was a habitual football gambler. It was growing more difficult to tell himself it wasn't a significant problem.

By this time he'd been disabused of any illusion of proving anything by his football wisdom. He was no more accurate in picking winners than he'd ever been. In everything else he could think of, practice made perfect. But when it came to betting, he now understood that the only consistent winners are the bookies and the odds setters.

There were weekends when Chip lost nearly every bet. And even when he won, it was never enough to cover his losses.

He worried about the marital tension his habit caused. Ava, like Jeremy, knew what was going on, but the gambling was a forbidden topic between them—something she disliked but was powerless to change.

And then there was the Ty factor. Ty was Chip and Ava's three-year-old son. Life and perspectives change radically once a little one comes into a home. Chip now saw every decision in a new light, and the betting habit was looking more insidious, unsustainable.

Someday, he told himself. *Someday . . .*

In clearheaded moments, he would think, *How could I let this thing go on and on? Why am I putting my home and my family on the line by betting on these games?*

But the next weekend he would hold the phone receiver in his hand again, think about it for just a moment, then place the call—place the bets.

Chip often thought, *Maybe I should ask Jeremy to help me.*

But he knew Jeremy would try to get him to stop gambling. And he *wanted* to stop—just not quite yet.

In early January 2009, college football was well into its season of bowl games. Some of the games fell on a Saturday when Ava was out shopping and Chip was home with Ty. The two of them watched the games together for a while, but the little boy wanted a little bit more action than sitting in front of a tube. TV football was incomprehensible and dull for him. "Daddy," he asked, "can we go outside and you can throw me the baseball?"

As January goes, it was a nice enough day. So father and son went outside to play catch. It could have been, should have been, a truly warm family moment—except Chip had lost several straight bets. He was concerned about another big loss, and all he could think about was the televised game.

Chip and Ty would throw the ball back and forth two or three pitches, and then Chip would say, "Hang on, Daddy needs to check something. I'll be right back." Then he would dash in to find out what was happening in the game.

Ty would sit in the grass and pop the ball back and forth in his baseball glove, waiting for Daddy. Even at age three, he knew this wasn't how the game was supposed to be played between father and son. On Chip's fourth trip indoors to check the score, Ty came right behind him.

"Don't you want to play catch?" asked Chip.

"It's no fun anymore," sulked Ty.

And that moment was almost enough. *Almost.*

Chip saw the disappointment on the face of a three-year-old. He also saw a father letting a crummy, destructive habit uproot the most sacred thing in his life—his relationship with his son. It was a sorry prospect.

All in the world my boy wants is a nice throw-and-catch with his father, and I can't give him that. I can't deliver on something so simple.

He's right, Chip thought. *This is no fun anymore.*

Lights and Voices

Chip brooded that day over letting his son down. But to his shame, he still wanted to win those bets. He was on a huge losing streak, in the hole several hundred dollars. If he could have just a couple of wins, maybe he could at least break even . . .

When Ava came back from shopping, tired but happy, she caught a glimpse of her husband's face and sized things up immediately. The bowl games were on, and this meant he was either going to be elated or in the pits of despair. She sighed and looked at Chip sadly but said nothing.

Chip still found a way to snap at her. "Just . . . don't look at me like that!" he barked. "I don't need that. Can't you just . . . go read a book or something?"

He was being ornery and unfair, and he knew it. He saw the hurt in his wife's eyes. Ty stood beside her, staring at his father.

"Ty," said Ava, "go play in your room, okay?"

Ty looked from one parent to the other, then did as he was told. There were no further words between Chip and Ava, but they both knew he was setting a bad example for his son. That hurt.

Still, there was the money. Chip had one more chance. He picked up the phone again, called the bookie, and placed the whole sum of the amount he was down on an NFL game. The Indianapolis Colts were playing the San Diego Chargers in an AFC play-off.

It was a late game, prime time, and Chip sat in the dark room and watched it by himself. Regulation ended in a tie. Chip's stomach was twisted in knots. If Peyton Manning and the Colts could come through for him in overtime, everything would be okay.

He believed in Peyton—no way the Chargers' Philip Rivers

was going to beat Peyton Manning at crunch time—and he said a little prayer, as people will do in watershed moments. It seemed as if the Colts held Chip Medders's happiness in their hands.

"Come on, Lord. Come on, Peyton. I just need three hundred dollars. One money TD pass. One fade in the corner of the end zone." He was standing, talking to the TV set.

But a Charger running back broke a big run, twenty-two yards, and San Diego won in overtime.

Chip collapsed into his chair and stared at the scenes of celebrating Chargers. He had lost a whole lot of money this time, but perhaps something more. He could sense that. He had blown an opportunity to be a good father, to be a good husband. Chip sat up in the chair and thought, *This isn't about the money. It's never been about the money.*

Chip walked to Ty's room and stood in the doorway, something that often calmed his emotions. He tried to make out the boy's sleeping form, but the room was pitch-black. Chip often enjoyed sleeping in his son's room—Ty loved it too—and this was a good night for that.

Chip crawled into bed, wondering what it was like to own the daily joy and innocent trust of a little boy. Then he settled under the covers and began his special blend of prayer and self-pity: "I mean well, Lord. I want to do better. Just get me that money back; that's all I'm asking. And if you'll do that, I'll . . ."

No use. He hated to hear himself throw the same pathetic, empty bargains at God. Who was he fooling?

He opened his eyes and found himself looking into the face of his son, bright as noon. It was as if a floodlight was shining on that face. Where was the light coming from? The rest of the room was still dark.

Then something happened that Chip would never have

predicted—for himself or for anyone else. He heard the voice of God.

To this day, it's difficult for Chip to discuss the event. He is an ordinary man with both feet on the ground, and he isn't given to visions, miracles, or voices from heaven. At the time, the very idea seemed crazy to him. Impossible.

But there it was. He was absolutely awake, there was a light on his son, and there was a voice in his ear:

Look upon your son. You denied him today, but you've denied my Son for your entire life.

That was all. The room was once more very dark and very quiet.

Chip sat up in bed and began to weep, overcome by what he had experienced. Suddenly the great questions of his life seemed as clear and as compelling as Ty's face had been just a moment before. The choices before him were stark and insistent. God's voice will do that to a person.

Chip wondered for a moment whether he should run and tell Ava. That was his first impulse, but he needed to think first, to work through this thing.

So he lay down again, stared at the ceiling until the sun rose, and thought about his life, his family, and his faith.

COMMITMENT

When morning came, Chip smiled to realize it was Sunday. It wasn't a bad time to get inside a church building.

He was still thinking, still processing, working on accepting the reality of what he had experienced in the still of the night. He decided not to talk to Ava about it—not yet—but he wanted to hear the music in the sanctuary, listen more carefully to the Scripture readings, and find out what the sermon would say to him.

The pastor's subject that week was guilt. Before beginning his sermon, the pastor did something unexpected. He invited any guilt strugglers to come to the front of the sanctuary and pray. Chip, a confirmed back-pew lurker, found himself up and walking. Ava took his hand and came with him.

There were about fifty people at the front, praying and recommitting themselves to lay their burdens on the sturdy shoulders of Jesus. Chip began to cry, and his wife watched him in wonder. It was no revelation to her that Chip had been at war with himself. She prayed silently that this would be the moment when her husband found his way home.

Chip couldn't stop the tears. His eyes shifted from Ava to the pastor, who was also crying.

Then, within his thoughts, the voice of God spoke again:

Look at your pastor. He weeps. He cries his heart out because he lost a son. Do you know how precious it is to have your child with you?

This was true. The previous year, the pastor's son had died of complications from a brain tumor. Chip considered the unthinkable pain of losing a child. He suddenly felt a deep impulse to go pull Ty from the church nursery and hold him close.

Then he thought again of God, who had also lost a Son.

It was all closing in on Chip. Still, he elected to keep his own counsel. He rose and returned to his seat, continuing to reflect.

As it happened, it was the first Sunday of a new year, and the day his church was starting a "Daniel fast," a twenty-one-day period of all-organic foods and no meat. Daniel in the Old Testament had prayed and fasted before God. Jesus, in the New

Testament, fasted for forty days in the wilderness in preparation for his ministry. Fasting is a way of disciplining and purifying the body in order to be more open to God's voice.

Ava had already told Chip she wanted to be involved in the fast and would be cooking accordingly. This meant that Chip, who loved his beef, pork, and chicken, would be forced into confronting the issues of his life every time he sat down at the table. And strangely, he welcomed the idea because he didn't want what had happened in Ty's room to go away. He didn't want his growing resolve to dissolve into the old slavery of bad habits.

Chip couldn't help but see all these forces gathering on the perimeter of his life, and he began to understand that he had no recourse but to run up the white flag, to surrender to what he knew was right. At the end of the fast, Chip Medders gave up his struggles and laid all the burden of his life and his anxieties at the feet of Christ.

He knew now that what he had called a "relationship" with Jesus was no more than a façade. Now he wanted the real thing, and he told God that. He made Jesus his master and knew that he had placed his very last bet. From now on he would be the husband and father his family needed him to be and the child his heavenly Father longed for him to be.

When Chip had finished praying, he immediately picked up the phone and called his best friend in the world. He told Jeremy the entire story, from the "night of the light" to the conviction that had come during the church service to the prayer of surrender he had just prayed. They had a long talk, and Chip came to understand that Jeremy had been patiently praying for him for fifteen years, the entire span of their friendship. Chip could hear Jeremy crying quiet tears of joy at the other end of the line.

Chip heard his own voice, the joy in it, and thought, *This is a new man. This isn't the person I've been for all these years. I'm really, truly changed.* And for the first time, he understood that "higher path" he had always felt that Jeremy walked. It wasn't about Jeremy at all. It was about the Holy Spirit coming to live within a man and bringing his life into the beautiful harmony it was designed to have.

The whole time that Chip and Jeremy had been friends, Jeremy had borne witness to his faith primarily through his actions. There's an old Christian quotation, often misattributed to St. Francis of Assisi: "Preach the gospel always, and if necessary use words." That describes Jeremy's approach with Chip. There is definitely a time for conveying the gospel verbally, but Chip, like most people, needed to see it in action first. For all these years, Jeremy had prayed for Chip and done his best to live by example.

Jeremy was a "walk the walk" kind of Christian. He believed words were cheap if there was no evidence of a transformed life to back them up. If he had ever grabbed his former assistant coach by the collar and started preaching hellfire and brimstone to him or nagged him about his gambling, the results wouldn't have been desirable, and Jeremy understood that. So he tried to live his message every day, trusting God to perform the "heart surgery" his friend needed that only heaven could provide.

When Chip finally hung up the phone, he went to find Ava. Her eyes were wide with curiosity when she saw him—because his were red with emotion. He sat her down and told her everything. Ava, a strong believer who read her Bible every day and kept a journal of her prayers, wept and hugged him tight. The things that happened in the private soul of her husband were the answers to years of her own prayers. God had to have done it, because she knew it hadn't been her or Jeremy or any other person. Chip was too stubborn; she knew that better than anyone. Who else but God could have broken through?

A few minutes after Ava and Chip finished their conversation, a text message arrived on Chip's phone from Jennifer Williams: "Welcome to the family."

GOD'S TIMING

From that day on, Chip and Jeremy enjoyed a deeper dimension to their friendship.

For fifteen years they had been like brothers. They had hunted together, coached together, and started families together. All those things were still important. But now they shared a life orientation, a strong commitment to their Christian faith.

The timing of these things was even more striking, because just as Chip found peace for his life and his home, Jeremy's family were facing the challenge of their lives. For several years now, Chip had watched as one of the healthiest men he had ever known slogged through a long process of doctors' appointments and medical consultations, only to be given a terrible diagnosis. Jeremy was still coaching, but he was steadily growing weaker physically. Increasingly, he needed help to get around, even in his own home.

Chip told Ava, "Jeremy was there for me for all those years. It never occurred to me that he was working with me the same way he worked with two thousand kids he has coached over the years. He did it quietly, he did it as a friend, but he pointed me to Christ the same way he did for all those players. He was strong for me, and now I think God wants me to be strong for him."

As Jeremy and Jennifer struggled with adversity, Chip would pray for them, encourage them, and send them little messages of comfort and hope from the Scriptures. One day, during an exchange of e-mails, Chip wrote these words to Jeremy:

> I went to Bible study last night as usual. We have been study-ing for the last several weeks about not only reading God's Word, but speaking God's Word. We have been focusing on handling adversity with Scripture. Last night God spoke to me about you. Something is about to happen to you that is going to be joyful news to all of us. I'm not sure what it is, but I heard God's voice telling me to have faith in him and a miracle was going to happen. Jeremy, I love you and want you to know how much my faith has been built upon your walk with Christ.

Chip had come a long way since he surrendered his life to Christ. He had been the principal at Manchester High School since 2007, a school that was burdened by great challenges of its own. There had been a 75 percent faculty turnover, with an extremely high level of learning challenge among its students. The stress of that job had once contributed to Chip's anxiety and his gambling problem. But now he found himself pouring him-self into giving those kids hope and inspiration, using all the lessons he had learned at Greenville.

He was also being asked to speak, to consult with other schools and educational groups, and to share his testimony in churches. Chip had always admired the way Jeremy could talk to kids about his faith, about that "higher path." He never dreamed that the day would come when he would have to take a stand when his friend and mentor could no longer walk, that he would have to bear witness for Christ when his inspiration could no longer speak.

Not long after he sent the e-mail to Jeremy about a coming miracle, Jeremy and Jennifer were contacted by ABC-TV on behalf of the popular show, *Extreme Home Makeover*.

Yes, Chip thought, the miracle came, right on schedule, and it was a good one. But it couldn't compare to the one he had seen lived out over the past fifteen years—the blessings in countless lives that came through the quiet faith of one man willing to make a difference.

13

A FRAGILE GIFT

As December 2002 arrived, it seemed as if the merriest of Christmases was in store. Jennifer was already humming carols.

Jeremy's rough but promising first football season at Greenville High had drawn to a close. He had never coached harder than he had that fall or experienced such a challenge—but then Jeremy thrived on challenge. At home, there was the special joy brought by Josie, who was almost eighteen months old.

Josie was the sunshine of their lives—toddling around the house, getting into everything, giving endless smiles for the low price of a few dirty diapers. Jeremy and Jennifer couldn't wait to show her all the decorations, to see her eyes light up as the Christmas tree did the same.

Not only that, but Santa had an extra-special gift this year: Jennifer was pregnant again. And she was very happy about that, very thankful to God.

Maybe it would even be a boy this time. Another girl would be terrific, of course, but one of each would be perfect.

As Jeremy and Jennifer drove to the appointment for her first ultrasound, Jennifer reflected on the experience of carrying another tiny human passenger inside her body. There was no feeling like it—the sacred responsibility of being a vessel for this new life. She was already anticipating the joy of holding and kissing the child for the very first time, the fun of watching little Josie as a big sister.

It was Tuesday, December 3, 2002. *The date of baby's first picture,* Jennifer thought. An ultrasound diagnostic image, of course, isn't a photograph in the strictest sense, but it does provide a "picture" of the fetus. If all went well, Jeremy and Jennifer would find out whether they were going to have a little boy or a little girl. The whole process fascinated Jennifer, who had a bachelor of science in education with a major in biology.

The sonographer ran the procedure, and Jennifer eagerly viewed the image, newly amazed at God's handiwork. She thought again of what the psalmist had written:

> For you created my inmost being;
> you knit me together in my mother's womb.
> I praise you because I am fearfully and wonderfully made;
> your works are wonderful,
> I know that full well. (Psalm 139:13–14)

Jennifer imagined herself sharing that verse with her little boy someday (for it was indeed a boy) as they looked together at this very picture. "This was *you* when God was preparing you in the womb," she would say.

But something caught her eye. "I don't remember this on my daughter's ultrasound," she said to the sonographer.

"What's that?"

She pointed to the image. "This line—right here, across the head. See?"

Jennifer waited for an explanation. Maybe it was just an artifact of the imaging—a stray bit of fluid, something like that.

The young woman was still for a moment as she studied it. Then she said, "Oh, well . . ." But she didn't finish the thought. Instead, she began moving around the room, picking things up, fussing with this or that, and finally hurried out the door. After the line had been pointed out, she hadn't made eye contact with Jennifer once.

The sonographer's behavior seemed a little strange, but Jennifer didn't want to leap to conclusions. She finished her appointment and she and Jeremy drove home, a little less cheery than they'd expected to be.

Pray for Our Baby

The next day Jennifer received a phone call from her ob-gyn. He was cordial and polite as he identified himself.

"Doctor?" said Jennifer. "I had a question about my ultrasound. There was a line—"

"Yes, I know," he said gently. "You're very perceptive, Jennifer." He paused. "The fact is, we do see some abnormalities on the image."

Jennifer held her breath. She waited.

"These could just indicate pressures on the baby's head from the uterus," the doctor said. "Just keep a positive frame of mind. We don't know much yet, but we do want you to come in for an AFP test."

"AFP?"

"Alpha-fetoprotein. It's a blood test that helps us screen for abnormalities."

"Doctor, what kinds of abnormalities?"

"It would do no good to worry about that. Or to worry about anything. Let's see what your blood says."

Jennifer went in for that test, praying all the way. But the moment the blood was drawn, she knew something was wrong. Her blood looked too dark; it was simply not right. At this point, the kind assurances of others didn't alter her conviction that something was seriously wrong with her unborn child.

The next ultrasound was scheduled for December 10, the following Tuesday. While they waited for the appointment and for the results of the blood test, Jeremy and Jennifer began asking everyone they knew to join them in prayer. "Pray for our baby," they said at first. "Pray for our baby boy."

But it didn't sound real, didn't sound personal, unless the baby had a name. This was a living human being people were praying for, even if they couldn't see him yet—even if he hadn't been born.

So the Williamses began saying, "Pray for *Jacob*." They had decided long ago that if they ever had a boy, he would be named Jacob. So now, months before his birth, little Jacob Williams became a real person to a great number of people, someone on whose behalf they'd gotten on their knees and cried out to God.

Jennifer's brother said that he had never prayed so much in such a short period of time. Aunts and uncles and cousins were praying. Friends were praying. Everyone at Edgewood Baptist Church was praying, as were several other churches in the area—everyone hanging on for December 10. At Greenville High School, some teenagers were saying the first earnest, serious prayers of their lives for the little son of their football coach.

At the next ultrasound appointment, Jeremy and Jennifer were surprised to be met not by the previous sonographer, but by someone who attended their church. It seemed like a little message from God: *Here is a fellow believer, someone you know. I sent her just for you.*

But the moment the ultrasound image appeared on the screen, Jennifer saw the tears in her friend's eyes. She said, "Excuse me for a moment, and I'll get the perinatologist."

That couldn't be good. Jennifer knew that a perinatologist is an obstetrician who specializes in maternal-fetal medicine, often working with high-risk pregnancies.

The perinatologist appeared and told Jennifer they were going to move her to their best, most accurate machine. When the image appeared on the new screen he watched quietly for a few minutes and then said, "Jennifer, I need to tell you that the little boy you're carrying has spina bifida, as well as a very significant amount of fluid on the brain."

Jennifer immediately began weeping. She had never been the stoic type, and this was not a stoic-type moment. She sobbed heavily as Jeremy tried to console her. "It's going to be all right," he kept saying. "We'll get through this, baby."

The doctor excused himself politely, giving the Williamses some much-needed privacy. After a few minutes he returned and pulled up a chair. Jennifer tried to take in the details without simply letting her mind shut down. "Your son has, I would say, an L1 lesion for spina bifida," said the doctor. "There is a severe amount of fluid on his brain, so we have to be concerned about mental retardation."

Jeremy listened carefully to the doctor's words. He didn't

have his wife's biology background, and he wasn't up on all the medical terminology. But he knew that his son was in grave danger and that his wife was overwhelmed with sorrow. He had to be the stoic one.

"Some infants with spina bifida are born without the chromosomes necessary for life," the doctor was saying. "Some of them simply die within days after delivery." He went on with horrifying details like this—each word summoning a nightmare from which Jennifer wanted badly to awake. Then the doctor came to his bottom line.

"Although I am a baby doctor, I have to tell you about the option of termination for your pregnancy."

Jennifer simply sat and listened, too much in shock to respond.

ONE IN A THOUSAND

Every year, about fifteen hundred babies enter the world with spina bifida—about one child per one thousand births. The term is Latin for *split spine*. It's one of the most common permanently disabling birth defects in the United States.

One of the most important functions of the backbone or spinal column is to enclose and protect the spinal cord and other vital nerve tissue. Spina bifida occurs when the bones of the spinal column fail to close properly around the cord while a baby is in the womb. The opening, which can occur anywhere from the neck to the sacrum, can allow nerve material or the spinal cord itself to protrude outside the spinal column or even outside the body, resulting in nerve damage and other disabilities.

All of this happens early in the pregnancy, often before the mother realizes she is carrying a child. Surgery after birth can repair the opening in the spine, but the damage to the spinal cord and nerves cannot be reversed. Physical disabilities are quite common, and mental disabilities of various degrees can also occur.

Some forms of spina bifida can be relatively mild, and the patient may see little or no effects to his or her life. The singer John Mellencamp, for example, was born with a mild form of spina bifida. But as the doctors informed Jeremy and Jennifer, their little Jacob showed signs of a more severe disability.

That same afternoon, Jeremy and Jennifer were to get the results of the blood test. Beforehand, there was time for lunch. They drove through a fast-food restaurant and took their orders to Lakebottom Park to eat. Neither spoke; neither tasted their meal. They could have been chewing on ashes. The two of them were processing their shock over what they'd been told.

The obstetrician sat down with them to share the results of the blood test, and at first, it sounded as if there was a ray of hope. The doctor said, "The blood work shows you have a one-in-forty chance of having a child with spina bifida."

Jennifer looked up quickly. "One in forty? That's not so bad—"

"Jennifer," he continued, "the normal figure is one in a *thousand*. This is just how blood tests work. These numbers, taken in tandem with your ultrasound, confirm to a certainty that you have a baby with spina bifida."

This doctor, like the first, now mentioned the option of "termination" of the pregnancy.

"Termination," said Jeremy flatly. "You mean abortion."

"Yes."

"No," said Jennifer, finally emerging from the mental cloud

that had enveloped her. "Abortion is not an option. Not for us. We're Christians."

The obstetrician smiled gently. "Jennifer, I can't pigeonhole people. I can tell you that what some people would never do to a healthy child, they will do to an unhealthy one."

Those words broke Jennifer's heart. Suddenly she felt the reality of the tiny, frail child who lived within her, who depended upon her for its very permission to live.

That little child was saying, "Can you love me? Can you love me anyway?"

And apparently some would answer, "No. I'm sorry. I cannot."

STRICKEN

For the next three days, Jennifer could barely function. She was stricken by sorrow and cried until it seemed there were no more tears to shed.

Jeremy had often said that in their relationship, she was the bucking bronco and he was the cowboy. She would stamp, leap, snort, and let it all out, and he would calmly try to rein her in, the way he reined in his own feelings. He was not one of those men who couldn't cry. But he understood there were the occasions when it was safe to do so and occasions when he had to be strong for someone else. In this case, his tears could wait.

Jennifer had always been fascinated by the story of John the Baptist in prison. John, the forerunner of Christ, had carried out an impressive ministry, preaching and baptizing thousands of people, but then he was arrested and thrown into a dungeon. He sent word to his cousin, Jesus, asking if he was indeed the Messiah about whom John had been preaching. It was as if John were asking, "If you are who I think you are, why is this happening to me?"

Jesus replied that he was healing the sick and preaching good news to the poor. And he added, "Blessed is he who is not offended because of me" (Matthew 11:6 NKJV). Jesus was saying you are blessed when you continue to follow him in spite of unmet expectations or disappointment.

There is a deep and blessed wisdom in humbly continuing to follow Christ when hardships come. Jennifer always felt that Jeremy had that kind of wisdom. He was the one who could handle heartbreak and not be "offended" by God. She would come around eventually, but she had to feel the offense for a while. She needed to shake her fist at the heavens and cry it out.

Jeremy was determined to be strong for Jennifer. But inside, a little piece of him was dying. It was the part of him that had harbored dreams of coaching his own son, buying his first soccer cleats, teaching him how to run the bases or chase down a receiver. Though he would not love his son an ounce less, it hurt to give up those dreams.

But he couldn't dwell on any of that yet. His role for now was to be a rock for his wife to stand on until she regained her strength. Both of them needed time to adjust to the realities that waited for them as parents.

The first night after the news, Jeremy came home with a thick sheaf of papers in his hand. He said, "Baby, look what I've got here. I've printed out all this information from the Internet, see? It's all about spina bifida. It's really not going to be so bad—we're going to be okay."

But Jennifer wasn't having any of it. "I can't read all that," she cried. "I just can't handle any of it right now."

I Will Carry You

On the third day after they got the news, Jennifer placed Josie into her car seat and drove to her grandmother's house, hoping to talk to her about what was happening. But when she arrived, she found that her grandmother had gone shopping. The world was still turning on its axis for other people. The sun was coming up in the morning. Stores were open. People were living their lives. It seemed very odd, though rationally she understood it.

Jennifer decided to wait for her grandmother to come home. She followed Josie as she toddled around the house. But the emotions just kept washing over her as she thought about the conversation they would have. All the pain came flooding back.

Then Jennifer simply hit bottom. She wept harder than she had before, moving about restlessly from one chair to another. She began pacing—picking up Josie, holding her close, putting her down again. Josie would look at her with those big eyes, questioning Mommy's strange behavior, then go back to her toys.

Finally Jennifer knew something had to give. She lay prostrate on the floor and began to cry out to God—not so much an ordinary prayer as a reflexive response of pain and terror, the response of a child bewailing the darkness.

"Lord, I cannot do this!" she sobbed. "*You* are going to have to carry me. I can't do this on my own!"

And at that moment, it was as if some unknown switch had been thrown deep in her soul. An amazing sense of peace and comfort flooded across her, a sweet aroma of the love and the presence of God. It was very real, and the tears simply stopped, drying upon her cheeks. Jennifer lay there for a moment, letting the warmth and the quiet seep into her. *It's going to be all right,* she thought. *God is going to be there.*

What is it about three days? Jesus struggled with death for three days in the tomb before his resurrection. Jonah prayed his heart out in the belly of a great fish for three days (though who knows how he kept track, with no view of the sun) before being coughed back up upon dry land. It's in the nature of grief that we're enshrouded in darkness, incapable of seeing the light. But there's something about that very darkness that can bring us where we need to be. Sometimes the end of ourselves is the beginning of God and the deepest experience of his reality.

> *When my life was ebbing away,*
> *I remembered you, LORD,*
> *and my prayer rose to you,*
> *to your holy temple. (Jonah 2:7)*

Jeremy arrived home that evening and Jennifer was . . . *herself.*

It was startling to him. It wasn't as if she was upbeat and happy. That would have been strange and even inappropriate. But his Jennifer was back. The strength and the resolve were back.

"I've been reading those printouts," she said. "Let's sit down and talk about them."

Jennifer still felt a deep sorrow for her unborn child and the challenges he faced—the challenges the entire family would face. But God had given her a solid assurance and a boldness she had never before experienced.

When life gets difficult, she realized, God gives. His grace is sufficient for whatever may lie around the next bend in the road, if only we'll cry out to him.

The Boy and the Beads

Jennifer still focused her efforts on asking everyone she knew—everyone at church, everyone she met—to "pray for Jacob." Now, however, the request came less from panic and more from a quiet strength and faith that God was working even in their challenging and troubling situation.

She would find herself in a conversation with, say, a cashier at the store. She'd say, "I don't know if you're the praying type. But if you are, and if you don't mind, I would sure appreciate your praying for Jacob, this child I'm carrying." She would then give a brief description of spina bifida and its threat to her little boy.

Nearly everyone she talked to was honored to be asked and promised to pray for the whole family. Jennifer could feel the power of so many people on their knees, interceding on their behalf before God. It was comforting and encouraging.

As time moved on, Jennifer felt something tangible was in order, something to symbolize the crisis and remind people to keep on praying.

As she pondered this, an event from the past flashed through her mind.

It was such a small thing—the boy and the beads. She began to smile at the memory, and her eyes filled with tears as she realized it had been God's provision before she ever knew the need.

Back in her teaching days, she had always possessed a determination to make her biology classes as hands-on and relatable as possible. She wasn't much for standing in front of anatomy diagrams and giving dull lectures. All that did was help a lot of her kids catch up on their sleep. So Jennifer had always been on the lookout for ways to make science more real and immediate.

One day she was teaching about the effects of ultraviolet radiation from sunlight on the skin. To illustrate her point, she produced a string of special UV-sensitive beads, which changed colors in the presence of sunlight. She held them near the window, where the sun came in, as a vivid example for her lesson.

After she had finished the demonstration, she passed the beads and little pieces of rawhide to all the students. She gave them a few minutes to experiment with the beads and then the students were allowed to make a bracelet or a key chain.

One of her students was a boy who had just arrived at school—a seventeen-year-old boy in a ninth grade class. Hardly anyone knew him or would talk to him. In hallway whispers, the word *thug* came up. He was a street kid, and no one expected him to hang around for long. And they were right; after two days he was gone.

But on one of those two days that boy happened to hear Mrs. Williams, the second-year science teacher, explain the effects of UV light. He was given a little piece of rawhide and a few beads and invited to make something out of them. And for whatever reason, the boy fashioned an attractive cross.

The sight of his handicraft, glowing with light from the beads, went straight to Jennifer's heart. She knelt down beside the desk and said, "That's so beautiful. How did you make that? Can you show me?"

And he did. He was clearly not someone who spoke much, but there was talent in his hands, and he seemed to become someone else as he worked.

That was all that happened that day, and for Jennifer the incident had faded into the dust of old memories. But now the memory had been nudged to the top as she thought about Jacob and prayer. Suddenly she visualized countless people carrying the little bead crosses as reminders to pray. She thought of the way the light of the sun would shine on the plain beads, changing their color to a lovely glow—a gentle reminder that Jesus is "the light of the world"—the "light of life" (John 8:12).

Jennifer bought beads and rawhide and began making little crosses, just as the boy had shown her, as fast as her hands could work. Jeremy learned to make them, too, and her parents and brother pitched in. They began giving the crosses away, and several recipients took a few extra to distribute. Soon you could see crosses everywhere. They were used as key chains. They were worn around necks or wrists. And whoever passed them along would say, "Be sure this helps you remember to pray for Jacob."

Jacob was born on April 17, 2003, the Thursday before Easter. He was a good, healthy weight, with no unexpected complications. In time, it became clear that his mind not only escaped any serious disability, it was bright, sharp, and witty. There were physical challenges, of course, and there would be a wheelchair in his future, when he was old enough and strong enough to sit in it. He would require constant care from his parents and, in time, his older sister.

Even so, Jacob brought incredible joy not only to his family but to everyone who came into contact with him. There was no way to be around Jacob without bonding with him, becoming his best friend. He could make the staunchest pessimist smile.

Jacob was an Easter season baby, and it showed. He would live under the constraints of a physical disability, but the very message and joy of Easter would shine from him. He had come into the world bathed in the prayers of countless people, and to see him, to talk with him as he grew older, was to realize that this world and its heartaches are only for a season. There is the blinding light of good news trying to burst out of the dull gray rags of this world. The gray is temporary; the light is forever.

Someday Jacob will awake, as we will awake, as a perfect creation, transformed in Christ for the coming life. His light will shine in rainbow colors we can't as yet imagine.

The medical journals said that Jacob was one in a thousand. But those who meet him say he's one in a million—or more than that. He is a fragile gift from heaven, but a precious one.

14

GUT CHECK

Life comes in cycles and seasons.

Marriage too.

The Bible says, "There is a time for everything, and a season for every activity under the heavens" (Eccl. 3:1).

After Jacob's birth, Jeremy and Jennifer found themselves in a new season of adjustment.

They had already been through a lot together. After those four years of waiting, they had delighted in becoming a married couple. They had enjoyed the camaraderie of working together and saving for their first home.

The arrival of Josie, their firstborn, deepened their joy but also propelled them into a new season of their lives. Jennifer now reveled in being a stay-at-home mom, while Jeremy was now the sole breadwinner. Fortunately, Jeremy was also becoming very good at his work in the world, at using his God-given gifts.

Manchester had confirmed that he was in the right line of work, but Harris County showed he could take the next step. As a defensive coordinator, he could get more into football's mental game: the Xs and Os, the breaking down of film, the exploitation of the opponent's weaknesses. He never tired of these challenges— which was a good thing, since he needed to put in more hours than he did at Manchester. He developed game plans and started a local weight-lifting competition. And he celebrated the fact that Harris County had made the play-offs for the first time in decades and had beat Manchester—something that almost never happened. At Harris County, Jeremy Williams really came into his own in his chosen trade.

Even so, when Josie was born during this time, Jeremy was involved in every part of caring for her. He fed her frequently, he changed diapers, and he was always there to watch her if Jennifer needed to be elsewhere.

But all that changed when Jeremy went to Greenville. Head coaching is an entirely different level of responsibility. It requires being the face of the program for the school and the community, managing the assistant coaches, and supervising both game plans, offensive and defensive. The head coach knows that several other salaries depend upon his, because if he is fired the next coach will probably hire his own assistants.

The buck stops at the desk of the head man. It's a big job anywhere. But at Greenville the pressure was multiplied. These kids needed more than game plans. They needed role models, encouragement, and a fair shot at being successful. Jeremy and his assistants felt a deep bond with them, something that went far beyond Xs, Os, and gridlines. Jeremy was becoming the father of many sons at the school just as he became the father of a son at home. And that reality, too, changed the dynamics of his marriage.

Jeremy was preparing for his team's breakthrough second season when Jacob was born. Between December and April, he and Jennifer knew their child would be born with spina bifida, so Jeremy had been as attentive as possible, supporting his wife and preparing for the birth.

But he still had to get his job done. His football family couldn't be overlooked. As a head coach of a struggling program, he simply couldn't be quite as flexible with his time as he'd been at Manchester or Harris County. He had to work later hours—supervising his assistants, building relationships with kids, manning the weight room, and putting in a brand-new kind of offense, which took extra time and study.

All this meant that Jennifer found herself with a little girl entering the "terrible twos," a tiny special-needs infant, and a husband she didn't see very much. In the best of circumstances, two little ones are far more challenging than one. But Jacob's needs and Jeremy's work demands made for a tough situation for a mother.

The truth was, Jennifer was lonely. Her day was fully dedicated to her kids, and she looked forward to telling Jeremy about their antics. She also longed for some adult conversation and a little help. But Jeremy usually would get home late and exhausted. Even when he was home, his mind was often elsewhere, caught up in one team issue or another. And that left Jennifer frustrated with this new season of their life together.

She knew Jeremy loved her and the kids. There was never any doubt of that. But she was also beginning to suspect that her husband, like so many career-oriented men, had become a workaholic.

FACING FACTS

After a particularly hard day, with both kids seeming to cry around the clock, Jennifer finally got them down and stepped into the shower. As the warm water sprayed across her face, she thought, *Now I can sleep until Jacob needs me. Then Josie will wake up, and I'll tend to her. Then, a couple of hours after that, another long day will begin.*

It seemed like an endless loop, a perpetual treadmill. Just thinking about it made her start to cry.

Someone once said that crying doesn't show that you're weak, but that you've been tough for too long. That's what was happening to Jennifer. It wasn't the first time she'd given in to frustration, but it was the first time Jeremy walked by and heard it.

He came into the bathroom, and the worry was evident in his tone. "Baby? Baby? What's wrong?"

She just kept crying for a moment as he tried to get a conversation going. Finally, wrapping herself in a towel, she said, "Jeremy? Are you happy?"

"Happy? Yeah. Sure."

"Not with football, Jeremy. Are you happy with us?"

Jeremy sat and looked back at her. In football terminology, he'd been blindsided.

"No," he said finally, quietly. "Not really."

"Neither am I. We love each other too much to let any of it slip away."

"I agree."

"And I don't want you to be one of those fathers who doesn't know his children."

Jeremy looked at her with real fear in his eyes. "I don't ever want that to happen, baby."

"So we have to do something to change it. I'm not going to survive without my knight. I miss you too much." Her voice trembled, and she tried not to start crying again.

"Okay, you're right. What can we do?"

They both thought for a minute, sitting there in the bathroom. Finally Jennifer said, "Remember that round-table thing? From Sunday school?"

They were active in a couples class at Edgewood Baptist. One day, during a conversation about relationships, the teacher had brought up the idea of a "round table discussion." It was simple enough. A couple was to sit together at the kitchen table, each with a pen and a sheet of paper, and each would make a list of five positive things about their spouse—plus one thing they saw as an obstacle that needed to be addressed. Then they would take turns sharing their lists.

The idea was strategic. Instead of waiting and letting bitterness build up and escape in the form of a big argument, why not be proactive and share issues, one at a time, in constructive context? The five positive items would provide a nice counterbalance for the harder truths.

Jeremy, the organized tactician, appreciated such a system.

They decided to wait until Saturday to do the exercise so they could pray and reflect first. They both enjoyed the process, taking turns sharing their compliments during the first section. When Jennifer got to her issue, Jeremy was ready to face it with a view to resolving the problem.

"Time," said Jennifer. "I'm a quality-time girl. My 'love language' is quality time." (Jennifer was well versed in Dr. Gary Chapman's book *The Five Love Languages*.[1])

"For me," she continued, "spending time together translates as love. Jeremy, I know how important your work is to you. It's important to me too! I want to support it in every way I can, and I would never get in the way of your doing your very best and doing the things you love."

She took his hand in hers and continued. "But what I would ask is this. After you've taken care of business, during those times when you have a choice of going home or doing extra—choose us! Choose the kids and me. If you have to get the game plan written, then you just have to do that. But if the choice is going over it a sixth time or coming home, come home. Choose us."

"Honey, I've been thinking about it since the other night," said Jeremy. "Over the last few years, I've been living my dream. I love coaching football. But I've put it first too often, and that's not right. God and my family are what's most precious to me. My work is secondary to those. And I promise you, we won't have to have this conversation again."

Jennifer fell into his arms and they just sat for a while. From that day on, their marriage moved on at a deeper and more committed level. Jeremy didn't simply try harder; he made changes in his lifestyle.

He did his work in such a way that there would be no problem coming home after a practice or a meeting. He also shortened practices on Thursday, which became a family night. Often they would meet at San Marcos, the local Mexican restaurant, and enjoy a meal out together. And on Saturday there would be no football—no watching of film, no getting together with his staff. That day completely belonged to family.

Jeremy didn't have a way to give Jennifer three more hours per day, but he knew he could give her thirty minutes. Those minutes added up, each one of them replacing a minute of frustration.

Meanwhile, Jennifer was trying some new things too. Months earlier, she had joined a play group for mothers with young children. Once a week the members would meet at ten in the morning to let their children play together. They might go to a playground or the pool, or they might plan some other activity. The moms could compare problems and find mutual support. It was a perfect outlet for the mothers as well as their children.

The changes Jeremy and Jennifer made in their lives to strengthen their marriage weren't always easy. They required tenacity and a certain amount of discipline, all in the name of love. But later they would realize that what they were going through was one more way God was strengthening their relationship for the trials ahead.

THE HAND THAT WOULDN'T HEAL

Such a small thing—a little tussle in football practice.

It happens all the time. Big guys line up against each other. One tries to block; one tries to get past the block. One tries to tackle; one tries to escape the tackle. Football is both a physical game and an emotional game, and that's a recipe for frustration and a little extracurricular contact.

Coaches know their players need passion to perform to their capabilities. Sometimes they need a little extra adrenalin to discover how well they can play.

One day in 2004, during spring practice, the Greenville coaches were working on a lineman who wasn't getting the job done. They were shouting at him, challenging his manhood, and trying to get a little smoke coming out of the ear holes of his helmet. They thought he needed a little nastiness injection.

So the inevitable happened. He finally crashed into his man with full force. The coaches were now shouting approval: "There it is!" "That's more like it!"

But the other guy didn't like being on the business end of

that day's lesson. He was tough too. He got up and took a swing at the player who'd hit him.

Soon Jeremy was getting between the players, cooling them down. This was a normal part of any football practice. But this time his left thumb got caught in the face mask of one of the players. He felt pain, winced, then decided it was nothing serious. As long as all five fingers were still there, well, he had a football practice to run. Tough players needed a tough coach.

Jeremy, like all players who have excelled at a high level, had a high pain threshold. Bumps and bruises and even worse were nothing new. Jeremy suspected he had torn a ligament between his thumb and forefinger, but that was okay. It would heal. The body was a hospital unto itself.

But as the weeks flew by and summer practice got underway, Jeremy noticed the hand with the injured thumb had gotten weaker. He wasn't feeling his usual fit self either. He had taken superb care of his body over the years, working with weights and striving to be as well conditioned as his players. But now he seemed to be losing strength in his grip.

Jeremy suspected he was dealing with more than an injured left hand, but he didn't want to stop and find out what it was. He was far too busy living his life.

Tripp Busby was beginning to worry about him. Jeremy's longtime friend was now a fellow Greenville coach. They met each morning to walk and talk, and Tripp noticed that Jeremy was always looking at his left hand, flexing it, prodding the muscles. He no longer seemed to have full control over it.

"Pray for my hand," Jeremy would say. He wasn't the type to admit fear, but his friend could hear it in his voice. He felt it himself. If Jeremy Williams could have a health issue, who was safe?

THE MEDICAL JOURNEY

During the spring of 2006, Jeremy rode his bicycle to meet his family at Callaway Gardens, a resort just outside of Columbus. When he arrived, he showed his hand to Jennifer. "Look at this," he said.

She was shocked by what she saw. The hand looked pink and mushy, like a piece of raw meat that had been pounded by the butcher's hammer. The atrophied area began at the thumb and extended across the hand.

"Jeremy, you *will* go to the doctor. I'll go with you. We can't ignore something like this. There's something seriously wrong with your left hand."

They started out with a specialist, a doctor who specialized in the hand and wrist. He seemed perplexed after examining Jeremy. "There's nothing actually wrong with your hand—at least, not structurally," he said. "No bone or ligament damage. This is very odd, really. I'm wondering if you could have a pinched nerve in your neck."

There was always the possibility that some old football injury was at the root of the problem. Four-year college players, who have made a considerable number of tackles and taken on thousands of hits, typically carry their physical history in their bodies.

At that point, more doctors had to be consulted. More X-rays had to be studied.

An orthopedic surgeon indeed found an old injury—a fractured vertebra, now healed. But there was nothing pinching; nothing to account for the mysterious hand problem.

During the summer of 2007, a neurologist administered a series of EMG (electromyography) tests to test muscle function.

By this time, the problem had extended to an increasing weakness in the arm. Jeremy felt himself gradually losing strength, first on the left side and then—the worst sign yet—on the right as well.

The neurologist said, "Jeremy, you either have a motor-neuron problem such as Lou Gehrig's disease—ALS is the medical designation—or what we call multifocal motor neuropathy—MMN for short. The diagnosis you really don't want is ALS, because there is no cure for it. So let's try treating it as if it's the less serious MMN. We'll try an immunoglobulin infusion."

Jeremy's head was swimming in medical terminology. None of it sounded very good, but he was willing to take on any medicine or therapy that would heal his body and get his life back to normal. With Jennifer's help, he began his treatments, which proved to be quite taxing. At the first football scrimmage of 2007, people were walking up and asking if he was well. Jennifer had never seen him looking like that—sweating, listless, and throwing up.

But then there was a ray of hope. After two treatments, Jeremy felt better. His hand seemed to be healing, his grip getting slightly stronger. After the dark clouds that had been forming over their family life, Jeremy and Jennifer were exhilarated. What a strange malady he'd had. But now, with the help of the immunoglobulins, things were going to get better.

After the third treatment, however, there was no improvement. Jeremy had to admit he was feeling weaker again. And after the fourth, fifth, and sixth treatments, it was clear that he was headed in the wrong direction. By the ninth treatment, Jeremy and Jennifer were beginning to seriously confront the possibility of the darker prognosis.

15

WE DO WHAT WE DO

THERE ARE TIMES WHEN WE BEAR UP UNDER THE WORST and then stumble over something small. Call it the "last straw" syndrome. It just seems as if when the big things aren't going our way, the little ones ought to fall into line. But that's not how real life works.

Jennifer had one of those moments in early summer of 2007. She was walking out to the barn to feed the horses, thinking about her husband and his weak, pulpy left hand, when she reached her own left hand into her pocket. Her engagement ring snagged on her robe, and when she pulled out her hand, she saw that her diamond was missing.

Surely it had to be right there within a few feet. But three days of searching couldn't locate it. It was simply *gone*.

In so many ways, this was a low blow at the worst time. Jeremy was obviously sick, and no one could tell them what was wrong. The treatments that seemed to be helping were no longer effective. And Jennifer was beginning to hear those whispers of doubt. Sometimes she couldn't help but ask, *Where is God in all this? Doesn't he hear our prayers? Why won't he heal Jeremy?*

Besides, though she'd once told Jeremy she didn't care about a diamond, Jennifer loved that ring. Jeremy had given a summer of hard labor to buy it for her, and that alone made it precious to her. It also reminded her of God's goodness and blessing in bringing the two of them together. Now, just as that togetherness was threatened by Jeremy's illness, the diamond had vanished into thin air.

Jennifer kept remembering a Bible study she had done that spring. Based on a book called *Restore My Heart* by Denise Glenn,[1] it focused on the eternal truth of Christ's love for his bride, the church. The study also went into great detail about the wedding ceremonies of biblical times. In those times, the ring was worn on the first finger of the right hand because people believed there was a direct connection between that finger and the person's heart.

Jennifer's heart, however, was broken, not restored. Her perfect man was in jeopardy. Her perfect stone was lost. Jennifer was distraught over the loss.

Jeremy understood. He never said, "Hey, it's just a ring." He recognized that to her, the diamond had come to symbolize their union. It reminded her that even if they were separated in life, they could never be separated in love. But now even the symbol had been snatched away. She had to cry out to God, *What's it all about? Why is this happening?*

On the fourth day after the ring was lost, Jennifer left for a family vacation and talked with her father. He thought about the problem and made a smart suggestion. "Search at night," he said. "Maybe the diamond will catch the rays of a flashlight."

Dads are smart. Jennifer was encouraged, and the second she got back home and darkness fell, she was in the backyard on a mission with the family's three dogs tagging along. But after an hour—nothing.

As Jennifer walked back to the house, she realized it wasn't just about the ring anymore. It was about the warfare that was going on in her heart. Couldn't she trust God in a relatively small thing like this?

Trust. She stopped halfway between the barn and the house, the word *trust* hanging in her mind.

Faith, someone once said, is walking to the edge of all the light that you have and then taking one more step. Jennifer stood in the darkness, physical and emotional and spiritual, and decided she would take that step.

"Lord Jesus," she said, "I'm simply going to trust you—and rest in that trust. If for some reason you don't mean for me to have my ring, then I accept that. I guess sometimes faith must go beyond insisting and just accept. So okay. I trust your love for me, no matter what. I don't know what's best for me, and you do."

Immediately Jennifer felt a great burden slip loose and topple from her back. She began to walk back toward the door of her home, shining the flashlight around and playing with the dogs. It felt good to have a childlike faith.

Suddenly there was a glimmer in the flashlight beam.

She had simply been pointing it anywhere and nowhere. And there, in the center of the back step, there was a dazzling point of light. Facedown, her diamond was waiting for her there.

Jennifer was sobbing like a baby as she ran into the house, babbling to her bewildered husband that God had returned her diamond to her.

Jennifer would come to feel that the diamond episode was all about a lesson she had to learn. God loves us, no matter what happens. We need to trust him, no matter what happens. Could she do that? Could she be faithful in the small things? Could she grow in wisdom so that the larger crises, which always come, would not destroy her?

A Time to Weep, a Time to Refrain

Jeremy wasn't getting any better. He and Jennifer continued to pray, and everyone they knew covered the family in their own heartfelt prayers. But there weren't any good signs, only an increasing array of medical consultations.

Finally, in October 2007, Jeremy and Jennifer traveled to Macon to see a specialist. Jeremy had actually been looking forward to the trip because there was a Bass Pro Shop nearby, and they had the kind of shoes he needed.

The doctor simply said, "I'm sorry, but you have ALS, Lou Gehrig's disease." His air of certainty was breathtaking in its futility. He continued matter-of-factly, "I want you to go see Dr. Glass at Emory."

Jeremy, who had argued with the judgment of many a referee in football, accepted this opinion quietly. But Jennifer fell to pieces. Jacob, age four, watched her as she sobbed, clearly wondering what was wrong with Mommy. But Jeremy just reached over, brushed away a tear, and said, "I still need those shoes."

Jennifer couldn't believe it. How could the man be thinking about shoes when he had just been handed what was, for all intents and purposes, a death sentence?

But Jeremy had his own way of handling things. There was a time to weep, as the book of Ecclesiastes said. But for him, now was not the time to open the floodgates.

They found the store and shopped for the shoes. Then they drove home in their separate vehicles—Jeremy in his jeep heading to football practice, Jennifer and Jacob in the truck. All along the highway, Jennifer's eyes were filled with tears. It was early afternoon. She knew Jeremy had to go to practice just as if it were an ordinary day. But she'd be left at home to her grief, to the knowledge that there would be no more ordinary days.

Jennifer was still a young woman. Her life had been a series of challenges, but she'd taken them on one by one and grown through each one of them. She had waited for Jeremy during those first three years of college. She'd made the adjustments to become a wife, a teacher, and then a mother. Most of all, she had prepared herself to be the mother of a special-needs child, a child who was constantly a blessing.

She had thought she knew all about weathering storms, that she'd learned a lot about trusting God.

Now she understood she'd had no clue.

If there was anything in the world she couldn't face, if she had any weak point, then nature had found it. She could not lose her Jeremy. She just could not.

The ride had put Jacob to sleep. She carried him gently into the house and tucked him into his bed. Then she stood in the doorway a moment, studying the soft, childlike innocence of his face and wondering, *How do I tell the children?*

Jacob, of course, was very small and would simply accept what was happening around him as life went on. Josie wasn't ready to be told. She would have to be acclimated to the terrible truth very slowly and deliberately. There was no need to talk about death right now. The children just needed to understand their father wasn't well—as Josie already understood—and that it would become harder for him to play with them over time.

But Jennifer couldn't face all these things right now. She would go crazy, she felt, if she tried. She needed to be outdoors, to find something to do with her hands. Anything but sit by herself and fight these waves of sorrow

There was a large chestnut tree close to the house. Little sticky burrs, thousands of them, covered the ground at this time of year. Raking wasn't one of her favorite tasks, so normally she just ignored them. But now she got after those sticky burrs with a rake in her hands and grief in her spirit, slashing away at the burrs as her tears continued to fall.

There was the sound of an approaching vehicle. Jennifer looked up. She heard tires hitting the gravel on their drive. It couldn't be Jeremy. At five o'clock, it was far too early for football practice to be over.

But it was Jeremy. He climbed out of the truck and took in the sight of his wife, her face red from crying, piles of burrs all around her.

"Babe," she said, "what are you doing home?"

He took her in his arms. "I came to be with you."

"But your practice . . ."

"I called Tripp and told him I wouldn't be there today. And then I drove up to Pine Mountain, up to Dowdell's Knob, just to pray a little bit. I'm fine now."

"Fine? How can you be fine? I'm not!"

"Let's go inside." He took her hand and led his wife into the sunroom.

Guard My Heart

Dowdell's Knob is a scenic area on Pine Mountain, another favorite spot of President Roosevelt's for solitude and reflection.

The legend was that Lewis J. Dowdell, one of the men it was named for, used to bring his slaves there for worship on Sundays. Somehow that high spot seemed closer to heaven—a beautiful place that reflected God's presence.

That's exactly why Jeremy had driven his truck up there. He had some things to sort out with God.

Up there on the knob, he cried out in anger and bewilderment, shaking his fist at the heavens. There was a fury in his soul, and he couldn't be dishonest about that. He thought about his wife, his precious children, his football players, his health—how could these things all be taken away from him? He sat and wept for a long time.

And then, when it seemed as if the tears had run their course, Jeremy asked God to take away his anger. Not his hardships, just his bitterness. He knew that hardships sometimes fit into God's plan, but bitterness never did. So that was his prayer: *Give me your peace, Father. Take away this rage.*

And just like that, God answered the prayer. Jeremy sat for a few more moments, allowing the peace to take hold of all that was within him—letting go of his resentment, his demands upon heaven. Then he began to praise God's name, worshiping from the heart. The more he worshiped, the stronger he felt.

He thought of what the apostle Paul had written: "The peace of God, which transcends all understanding, will guard your hearts and your minds in Christ Jesus" (Phil. 4:7). *Guard my heart,* he prayed. *Guard my mind. Give me the strength to tend to my family.*

At that point, he had driven home. Now he ushered his wife into the living room. He sat in a chair and she sat on the floor, leaning on her husband's knees, starting to cry all over again as he rubbed her shoulders.

Gently he told her, "Babe, we're going to take this one day to cry. Then, tomorrow we're just going to keep doing what we do."

GOING DOWN FIGHTING

Jeremy spent the next day adjusting his game plan. That's how he looked at it.

A football coach scouts the opposition. He watches film of the opponent's offense, defense, and special teams. Then he creates a plan for engaging and defeating the opponent, and he coaches his team on that plan.

Sometimes, though, a coach needs to make halftime adjustments. The other team may be doing something he didn't expect—blitzing the safety or attacking a certain weakness. A good coach addresses these challenges quickly so he'll have an answer in the second half.

Jeremy was facing the toughest opponent of his life now, and he knew he needed to adjust his game plan. He thought, *Am I going to fade away quietly, with the devil laughing at me? Or am I going to allow Christ's strength to be seen in my weakness, giving God all the glory?*

He knew the answer to that one. Jeremy Williams had always loved a challenge. He was going to be all in for what God wanted to do through this trial.

He thought of a line that Jennifer had mentioned to him often. She'd heard it from an evangelist named David Ring. Jennifer had never forgotten the man's testimony. The man had been born with cerebral palsy, orphaned by age fourteen, had a speech impediment, and walked with a limp. But he said,

"When I wake up in the morning, the devil shudders with fear. What does he do when you wake up?"

For Jeremy, as he looked at the onset of ALS, those words really had power. He wasn't going to cower or complain. He was going to take his stand and let the devil be the one to run for cover.

Nor would he let this crisis be all about him. So often, when a serious challenge comes along, we become self-absorbed people. We close up and privatize our struggle—which, of course, is precisely the opposite of what we should be doing. Jeremy didn't want that at all. He saw his medical situation in the greater context of spiritual warfare.

For example, he was acutely conscious of his team and his responsibility to influence his players in a positive way. He simply couldn't let ALS keep him from that mission.

Even before his trip to Macon, the 2007 football season had opened in a strange way. The Patriots had won their first two games, but Jeremy felt that all was not right with his squad. The team was lacking in character. So he had actually prayed with the team that most uncommon of prayers, the request for adversity. *Give us something to fight, Lord,* he'd said. *Give us some kind of obstacle to overcome so we can become stronger men of character.*

The answers to that prayer came quickly. First, the team lost the third game in a heartbreaker—by one point to the number-one team in the state. A Patriot dropped the ball as he crossed the goal line. (The team would finish its season 4–6, the second worst year of Jeremy's coaching career.)

The following week, a couple of players got into trouble— just the kind of character indicator that Jeremy had seen coming. These players had to be suspended for two games.

And then, far worse, the team's quarterback lost his father, a man well loved by all the players, in a traffic accident.

Jeremy felt all these events as spiritual attacks. As far as he was concerned, this was war. And it was at this point that he had traveled to Macon with Jennifer and Jacob to hear the pronouncement that he did not have a superficial medical problem. He had a progressive, guaranteed-fatal condition called Lou Gehrig's disease.

He had gone to the mountain and had his confrontation with God. He'd made the decision that, if he had to go out, he was going to give the devil as much grief as possible on the way. And it would begin that very day at practice, when he talked with his team about what was going on.

For the players it was just another autumn day, another football practice. Jeremy called the team together and said, "Guys, I told you I'd keep you posted on my health situation. Well, it's terminal. I'm going to die, maybe in two years, maybe in five or six. Okay, let's go practice!"

Needless to say, the players were shocked. They had no idea how to respond. It was less than a crisp and enthusiastic practice. Teenagers don't process death announcements quickly. Who does, really?

Jeremy was disgusted with the lethargic effort he was seeing. Then the team chaplain, Gerald Fowler, walked up to him. "Hey, Coach," he said. "You can't just lay something like that on kids and expect them to act like nothing's wrong. You have to talk to them a little. Call a break soon and give me a shot."

A few minutes later, Jeremy called for a water break. As the team stood around drinking their water, Coach G, as he was known, said, "Listen up, men. What Coach told you is true. He got a tough report from the doctor, and he knows—we know—that his time is limited. But I know this: Coach could do a lot of other things with that time. He could spend it with his family. But he loves you guys. He loves you, and he has chosen to come out and give you this time.

"So you need to pick it up, right? Do your job! Make it worth Coach's precious time. All right?"

"All right!" shouted the team.

From there, it was the best practice the Patriots had ever had.

After the team was dismissed, Jeremy and Coach G were walking up the hill together—a task that would grow harder for Jeremy by the day. Coach G wrapped an arm around his friend's shoulders and said, "You know you've got my prayers, brother. But if you ask me, the devil always goes one step too far."

"Yeah," Jeremy replied, "and this time, all he's done is piss me off."

After that day, he paid much more attention to a program of bringing in a Fellowship of Christian Athletes speaker each Thursday in the field house. The great theme was always character: Who are you going to be in life? What do you stand for?

He posted Bible verses in the weight room and encouraged players to meditate and memorize as they worked out. And he recommitted himself to praying for every player by name each morning.

At the same time, Gerald Fowler noticed, Jeremy dialed up the discipline on his team. This had been a hallmark of the great Greenville turnaround several years earlier. Since then, he had been more hesitant to remove players from the team because he really wanted to make a difference in every life if possible. The troubled kids, he reasoned, were simply the ones who needed Christ the most. How could he send them away?

Yet now he realized he had to think in terms of team unity,

what was best for the group. There's truth in the old saying about a bad apple or two spoiling the barrel. So Jeremy modified his approach to discipline issues, especially when the 2008 season began. He still did everything he could to reach out to the troubled and the troublemakers. But if they would not respond, and if they became distractions to the team's character building, they had to go.

The remaining players began to respond positively to the renewed team discipline. They knew their coach was serious, and they became serious in response. The team was growing spiritually and, incidentally, playing better football. The 2007 season had finished at 4–6. The 2008 record would be 8–2, followed by a first-round loss in the play-offs.

All through this time, Jeremy had the strange sensation of knowing that his spirit was growing stronger each day, even as his body grew weaker. He remembered the words that Paul the apostle had written:

> But [God] said to me, "My grace is sufficient for you, for my power is made perfect in weakness." Therefore I will boast all the more gladly about my weaknesses, so that Christ's power may rest on me. That is why, for Christ's sake, I delight in weaknesses, in insults, in hardships, in persecutions, in difficulties. For when I am weak, then I am strong. (2 Cor. 12:9–10)

Jeremy Williams wasn't backing down. He was going to see just how strong in the Lord he could be while weak in the flesh. Not that the devil was going to give up easily; no, it wasn't that simple. But Jeremy was going to give him something to worry about each morning he was allowed to awaken on this planet.

16

WELCOME TO THE FRONT LINE

IN JULY 1938, THE "PRIDE OF THE YANKEES" WAS GETTING worried. Why was he so tired all the time?

Lou Gehrig was having another strong season, though his batting average and home run total, both massive in '37, were dipping a bit. Until recently, he had been baseball's greatest player. Now, for no apparent reason, he was becoming ordinary. No matter how much he tried to rest, he couldn't be refreshed.

As the 1939 season began, things went from bad to worse. He was stumbling on the base paths, and the power was gone from his bat. At age thirty-six he was still a young man, one of America's heroes. But just before a game in May, he approached his team's manager and removed himself from the lineup. He had appeared in 2,130 consecutive games, earning for himself the nickname of the Iron Horse.

Gehrig's longevity record would last for half a century. From June 1, 1925, until this game in 1939, he never missed an appearance. He played through taking a pitch to the head, several fractures, and a struggle with lower back pain that may have been the first true symptom of his disease. But the day finally came when he just couldn't play through, so he stopped.

Shortly afterward, Gehrig and his wife, Eleanor, checked into the Mayo Clinic, and there they learned that Gehrig had a rare and incurable motor-neuron disease called amyotrophic lateral sclerosis. His mind would not suffer, said the doctors, but his central nervous system would slowly deteriorate. His life expectancy was about three years.

On June 21, 1939, the New York Yankees held a day of appreciation for its ailing player. While Babe Ruth and other Yankee legends looked on, Gehrig stepped to the microphone and said he considered himself "the luckiest man on the face of the earth." It was a famous American moment, the words echoing dramatically through the stadium.

Gehrig lived for two more years and, in the process, became more than a baseball legend. Because of him, an obscure and mysterious disease took on a human face, because everyone in America knew about Lou Gehrig. Now they knew about the insidious condition that had felled the Iron Horse but couldn't destroy his courageous spirit. Though the disease had been reported in medical writings as far back as 1824, the condition was never well known until the world watched the tragic decline of one of its favorite athletes.

ALS is caused by degeneration of nerve cells in the central nervous system. These are the neurons—messenger cells from the brain—that allow us to control how we move our muscles. As these neurons begin to fail, messages no longer go back and forth between the brain and the muscles in the upper and lower body. And since we can no longer guide our muscles, they begin to weaken, or atrophy, from disuse. It all happens a little at a time until nearly all muscle function is lost.

There was a strange symmetry in Jeremy falling victim to a disease named for an athlete so similar to himself. Lou Gehrig was clean-cut, a team player, an overachiever who always saw the bright side of things. Like Jeremy at Memphis, he had seized an opportunity to play his position when a teammate wasn't available. Both men were opportunists, playing too well to return to the bench. And finally, each man accepted his prognosis with uncommon courage, smiling and encouraging others in the face of unthinkable tragedy.

Lou Gehrig saw himself as the world's luckiest man.

Jeremy Williams saw himself as someone with an opportunity to glorify God.

At first, his wife was incredulous about that attitude. "How can you take it like that?" Jennifer asked. "I can't do it—I'm too mad. I just don't understand . . . why you? Why should this happen to a person who has such a strong impact on young people for Christ?"

Jeremy replied, "If I can handle it, you can handle it. Just turn it over to Jesus. Put it on his shoulders, and he'll give you the courage."

"It's not that easy, babe. It's just not. You are my knight."

They flew to Baltimore to get another opinion at the Johns Hopkins Hospital, and the specialist there agreed that Jeremy had ALS. Dr. Jonathan Glass of the Emory University ALS clinic in Atlanta also confirmed the worst.

So the path ahead was very clear. It was simply a matter of how to walk down it. Jeremy and Jennifer would find their courses in very different ways.

"No Different Than You"

During the summer of 2008, Jeremy was invited to speak at a Fellowship of Christian Athletes camp held at the University of West Georgia in Carrollton, Georgia. He was bringing twenty of his players to the camp, hoping and praying they would connect with Christ during the time with speakers, coaches, and other players. More than a thousand were expected. It was one of FCA's big events. The people of Greenville had donated the money for the students to attend because they believed in Jeremy and who he stood for.

Jeremy was scheduled to come to the podium just prior to the featured guest. He sat in the back of the room, trying to prepare himself to speak to such a large audience. He had made the nervous decision to open up and share about his ALS during the testimony. But he'd never talked about it in that kind of venue. He knew it would be difficult to keep his emotions in check as he spoke about his future and his health and his family.

The speakers at these camps were usually well-known figures. No one had really heard of Jeremy Williams, the guy who was scheduled to go on right before the main attraction. In introducing Jeremy, the host told everyone they were about to hear from a coach who had a terminal illness, and he called on everyone present to pray for that coach right now.

Jeremy came forward and knelt as hundreds of other young men—athletes and coaches—came forward, laid hands on him, and prayed for him—a huddle five-hundred football players strong, gathered at the feet of Christ to minister to a brother. Jeremy hadn't expected this, and he was deeply humbled. He dissolved into tears, feeling all kinds of emotions breaking loose within him.

It was a powerful experience, a transforming experience. The only problem was that Jeremy was supposed to follow it up by speaking to the crowd. That was simply impossible with his mind and emotions in such turmoil.

Yet God specializes in the impossible. Almost instantly, as he climbed the platform, he felt "the peace of God, which transcends all understanding" (Phil. 4:7) coming over his spirit like a blanket. And then he felt a fire in his heart, a consuming fire that compelled him to testify in the name of Christ.

Jeremy stepped to the microphone and said, "Yes, I'm Coach Jeremy Williams. And I have a disease called ALS, which you might have heard about under the name of Lou Gehrig's disease. I'm going to die in two years, or four years, or maybe eight years. And you know what? That makes me no different than you. Because you're going to die, too, possibly even in that same time frame. You don't know when. You just know it will happen."

Jeremy had been to FCA camps before, and he knew the drill. This worship service always came after a long day of practices and squad games, and the room was filled with tired bodies. It wasn't unusual to see half lidded or even closed eyes during the speaking periods. But that wasn't what Jeremy saw now. He saw a room filled with alert faces, kids leaning forward, hanging on to every word as if their lives depended upon it. Because as Jeremy told it—their lives did.

"I may be on my way out," Jeremy told them, "but I know exactly where I'm going. And I know whose team I play for. How about you?"

The words flowed from him as if they weren't even his own. Jeremy, who loved challenges, threw one out to the room. "Don't just play for wins, for banners, for rings and fame," he said. "Play for something eternal; something that never passes away. Play for God's kingdom."

Gerald Fowler sat with the Patriot delegation that day and marveled at the way the Spirit of God was moving through that room. There was an electricity in the air that brought the unmistakable feeling of God's presence.

Jeremy talked about college ball, about being a little guy who was somehow known as the "Georgia Assassin." He was a warrior, and a warrior on the field could also be a warrior in the spirit. He quoted the New Testament: "We are hard pressed on every side, but not crushed; perplexed, but not in despair" (2 Cor. 4:8).

"I am a warrior for Christ," he said. "I'm hard pressed but not crushed, and I will *not* go quietly."

As Jeremy walked off the stage, he was startled to hear a roar from the crowd—a spontaneous victory cry you might expect in the final seconds of a championship game. Up until then, the room had been absolutely silent apart from Jeremy's voice. As Jeremy passed them on the way to his seat, young men with tearstained faces reached up for high-fives.

Jeremy felt as if, when he was at his weakest, Jesus had taken hold of that moment and filled him with strength for the sake of those in the room. Jeremy sat and he wrote down five names and prayed for them. These were names of players he'd brought along, young men who needed to become followers of Jesus Christ.

When the featured speaker finished his own presentation and invited everyone there to come forward and receive Christ, Jeremy closed his eyes and prayed again for his five names.

When he looked up, he saw that an old-fashioned revival was in process. Kids were streaming down the aisles to accept the invitation. Jeremy scanned the faces and counted one, two, three, four, and then all five of the players he had brought before

God. There was even a "bonus"—a young man who was just a freshman, so that Jeremy hadn't yet known his spiritual situation.

He sat back, wiped a tear from his eye, and offered his gratitude to heaven for letting him be part of such a miracle. When he first learned about the ALS and revised his game plan for life, the most specific part of that plan had been to seek speaking opportunities to give his testimony and encourage people in the name of Christ. Now he saw just how powerfully God was answering that prayer. His weakness was just a vehicle for God's strength.

At that moment, he realized that ordinary lives were highly overrated. None of these things would be happening if he lived an ordinary life. He served an extraordinary God, and he couldn't wait to see what surprises were to follow.

He could never have imagined them in his wildest dreams.

Taming the Bronco

While Jeremy was pointed squarely at the future, his wife was still fighting it. Knowing she was a lover of horses, Jeremy again called her a "bucking bronco"—someone who heaved, chafed, snorted, and refused to accept what she was saddled with in life.

"Give Jesus the reins," Jeremy kept saying. And Jennifer was trying to do that.

Again.

When she had learned she would give birth to a child with spina bifida, she had fought with God at first. But it had taken no more than three days for her to subdue her spirit and trust the goodness of her Lord again.

Now was different. This was too much, and God knew it. Jeremy was the focal point of her life, her anchor, her everything.

You might as well take water from a fish as to take Jeremy away from Jennifer.

She didn't want to be consoled. She didn't want to be shown any Bible verses. When the sermons and the advice and the truisms began, something inside her switched off and she refused to listen. She *wanted* to hold on to her anger.

She did try at times. She prayed that God would remove her rebellion, her rage. She asked for the firm sense of direction that her husband had. But her prayers seemed to bounce off the ceiling. Heaven was silent. She missed her relationship with Christ. But at the same time, she wanted to know where he'd been when she needed him.

For just over a year, Jennifer wandered in a spiritual wilderness. It was the toughest period of her entire life. There were days when she thought she was close to God, then the next day she would feel swallowed by the emptiness again.

One day, sitting beside Jeremy in Sunday school and listening to their teacher, Jonathan, she heard a lesson taken from a Bible passage (Hebrews 11) about the great heroes of faith in the Old Testament. Abraham, Isaac, Jacob, and Moses were different individuals with varied accomplishments, but they all held one thing in common: a faith that pleased God. Each one pursued God's promises, even when the reality of those promises couldn't be seen by human eyes. They staked their lives on the reality of God and the certainty of his promised rewards.

And yet the writer of Hebrews says of these great men of faith:

> All these people were still living by faith when they died. They did not receive the things promised; they only saw

> them and welcomed them from a distance, admitting that
> they were foreigners and strangers on earth. . . . They were
> longing for a better country—a heavenly one. Therefore God
> is not ashamed to be called their God, for he has prepared a
> city for them. (Heb. 11:13, 16)

Jennifer was caught short by these verses.

These people from the Scriptures had died without receiv-
ing all that God had promised them. More than that, they'd
passed on without learning how all God's promises would
be fulfilled in the greater promise of Jesus Christ. But their
lives weren't governed by disappointment, but by hope. They
were people of faith, and therefore God says they were his kind
of people. When God brags on you in the Bible, that means
something.

That lesson got her thinking more deeply about her situation.
Then, not long afterward, she happened to watch a DVD fea-
turing the pastor and speaker Louie Giglio. The title was *Hope:
When Life Hurts Most.*[1] Giglio was speaking on the motives of
the heart—the ones we're reluctant to admit. Most of the time,
we're just focused on avoiding pain and finding comfort.

That resonated with Jennifer. She realized that she had
thought her goal in life was to honor God and lead others to
Christ. But that was a lie. Her actual goal was to get herself and
her family as far down the road of life as possible without anything bad happening.

The heroes of Hebrews were content to travel down a road
that often brought pain. Jennifer wanted to walk that road only
when the weather was nice.

And she knew that God couldn't use someone like that.

HOW GOD SPEAKS WHEN
WE'RE NOT LISTENING

Finally, God spoke to Jennifer through a novel she was reading. *Adam* was a thriller with a spiritual twist by author Ted Dekker. The back of the book contained a conversation between Dekker and fellow author John Eldredge on the subject of spiritual warfare.

Why, Dekker asked, do so many Christians give in to defeat when they know they're already victorious through Christ?

Eldredge replied that Christians tend to make a crucial mistake: They fail to fight fire with fire. Spiritual battles must be fought with a spiritual arsenal. For example, Jesus defeated Satan in the desert using nothing but Scripture. Paul handled his suffering with prayer. Neither of these tried to reason or emote their way out of their challenges.[2]

This understanding turned out to be the last piece in a divine puzzle, the key for helping Jennifer return to her Lord.

It was remarkable really. Jennifer had been avoiding the Bible, and she had little appetite for prayer during the months when Jeremy's ALS was verified. She had basically cut herself off from God. Yet what had God done? He had reached out to her through a Sunday school class, a DVD, and a thriller novel.

God, she realized, is faithful to us. He will use other believers who seem to cross our path at a precise time. He'll use some little fragment of a sermon on the radio. Whatever it takes to penetrate our thick skulls, he'll use. God is patient. He keeps speaking until we listen.

Jennifer was humbled to realize how gently and persistently God had led her back into his arms. She was ready to start healing now. And just as Jeremy had devised a game plan, Jennifer now began to form a battle plan of her own. She realized the only way she could find rest for her troubled soul—the only way she could be useful to God again—was to take up the spiritual weaponry God made available to her.

What were those weapons? There was prayer, of course. There was the reading of the Word. But the very name of Jesus also held power over a tough moment. Jennifer learned this from the Christian author Beth Moore. When she felt under attack, she could say, right out loud, "I trust Jesus!" Then she would feel a surge of his strength and courage.

In time, she had the courage actually to rebuke Satan in the name of Jesus. And for the first time she understood what Jeremy meant when he spoke of being a warrior rather than merely a sufferer. Why take all the blows? The best defense is a good offense.

There were times when Jennifer was so tired, so discouraged, that she'd simply speak the name of Jesus into her surroundings, over and over. She also learned to quickly turn to her Bible for guidance and comfort. It seemed as if every time she turned those pages, her eyes would fall upon a verse that seemed custom made for her need. She'd be anxious, and there would be a verse telling her that God had not given her a spirit of fear. She'd be feeling sorrow, and the Scriptures would counsel her in the true source of joy. When she felt abandoned, she'd come to those incredible verses in Romans (8:31–39) that explained how nothing—not trouble or hardship or persecution—could separate her from the love of God.

She found herself smiling when that happened. It was as if the Bible had been saving up verses for her during her long time away from it.

Jennifer knew she was well into the process of healing when

God began to use her once again to encourage others. Jennifer's cousin Amber was a first-year teacher at North Gwinnett High School. One day Amber called seeking advice on how to handle a situation with a troubled student. Jennifer began to encourage her using her own experiences from teaching. Jeremy was in the room, listening to the conversation.

When Amber asked for Jeremy's thoughts, he said, "Amber, welcome to the front line." He spoke to her as one who knew what it was like to go to battle for a troubled teenager.

Jennifer thought back to July 2008, when Dr. Glass at Emory had given the final confirmation that Jeremy had ALS. She had begun to weep once more, but Jeremy had simply smiled.

Welcome to the front line.

Those words made all the difference in the world. Everyone in this life is under attack. Everyone is a target of enemy hostility. But only some choose to be warriors, to equip themselves with the power of a strong and loving God and fight back with tenacity. Those soldiers may shed a few tears, they may suffer a few wounds, but ultimately they will smile, reach deep into the reserves within their soul, and take up the battle. And they'll know that God "is not ashamed to be called their God, for he has prepared a city for them."

Jeremy and Jennifer now had a warrior marriage. They fought side by side, and they fought to win.

17

A SEASON FOR MIRACLES

MOST OF THE LOCAL FOLK AGREED THAT IT WAS LIKE something out of a fairy tale.

People talk about Cinderella teams. Cinderella was the shabby girl who scrubbed the floors until the day the magic came—the day she went to the ball and found her prince. The forgotten team that somehow makes the postseason is always called a Cinderella team.

But there's also Sleeping Beauty. She's the one who fell asleep for many years, only to be awakened by a kiss from the handsome prince. Some teams are like that too. They seem to slumber for years before the right prince comes along and brings them back to life.

Greenville had its fairy-tale year in 2009. It was the sleepy little town that woke up and did something great. It was the dusty blue-collar squad that decided to put on its fancy clothing and go to the ball. In 2009, under Jeremy Williams's leadership, Greenville woke up, dressed up, and stepped up to a magical season.

Twice, during the 1980s, Greenville had won state championships. But that had been a quarter of a century ago—another lifetime, another Greenville. The class of 2009 hadn't even been born then.

Since then, hard times had only become harder in Meriwether County. Two hundred jobs had left home when Lanier, a clothing company, closed. Another hundred had vanished with a lumberyard that picked up and relocated to Alabama. There wasn't much left for building a career, supporting a family, cherishing a dream.

Fewer than a thousand residents now called Greenville home, and fewer than four hundred students were enrolled at the high school. Even James Bray, the mayor, had an Atlanta job. But like so many in Greenville, he loved his hometown. He wanted to see it come back to life. And it would be nice to see that happen on the gridiron, where Greenville competed with its town-and-country neighbors.

It had been a biblical period of seven years since Jeremy Williams came to town, and a lot had happened in that time.

After that rocky 1–9 start in 2002, things could only get better. And they did, in ways that were exciting and joyful. The players were better disciplined. They were working hard at strength and conditioning during the off-season. And sure enough, 2003 brought the unforgettable 8–2 turnaround—seven more wins than the season before, and many of them by lopsided scores against opponents accustomed to using Greenville as a doormat.

Those were great times. The stands were starting to fill up at the football games again. Jeremy made friends around town and preached the message of community support not just for the team but for the school—for the kids and their future. If Greenville football was ever going to achieve its potential, the school and the town had to join hands and believe in themselves.

The 2003 season at least removed the opportunity for

excuses: "We don't have the facilities. We don't have the large student body to draw from. We don't have the rich fan base." Jeremy and his coaches weren't going to accept any of those.

During the next few seasons, however, the message began to lose a little of its sheen. Greenville's record slipped to 5–5 for three consecutive years and then to 4–6 in 2007. Jeremy was still working hard; he was still building character in his players. But the team needed to be winning more games, and he was determined that was going to happen.

The problem of discipline reared its head again and again. Many of the kids on the teams didn't have a father in the home. They lacked male authority figures, and too many of them ended up getting into trouble with the school, the community, or even the law. Jeremy tried to reach every single one of them. He took many of them under his wing as personal projects, providing mentoring and counsel.

But the time came when Jeremy realized he was spreading himself too thin. Those who refused to reform had to be cut loose for the good of the team. And when Dr. Glass told him his health was on a downhill slope, Jeremy's sense of urgency spiked.

He only had so much time to accomplish something with his kids in Greenville. And he wanted to do a lot more with them than show them how to finish 4–6.

The Meaning of a Team

This was the time period when Jeremy stepped up his emphasis on character and discipline, when Jeremy and the core of his team had their remarkable experience at the FCA camp at West

Georgia College. After that, Jeremy began praying every single day, by name, for every player and every assistant coach. He also brought in inspiring speakers on Thursdays. Many of them were former Patriots. Some recounted the poor choices they'd made in the past, urging the players to do better. Others told success stories. Nearly all of them shared the gospel, describing that void in the human heart that can only be filled with Jesus Christ.

As the character training continued and a few disruptive elements were sent away, the rest of the team began to unite behind its ailing coach. The atmosphere around the team began to change in a way that everyone could feel, even if they couldn't quite articulate it. The players were stepping it up. They saw the fire in their coach's eyes, they felt the reality of his daily prayer for them, and they knew how much he cared for them. And they knew exactly how to show their gratitude. Whatever it took to bring home a championship season for their head coach in 2009, they were going to do it.

Jeremy suppressed any old-fashioned "win one for the Gipper" talk. In fact, whenever people talked about performing for Coach's benefit, he grew upset. This was not about him, he insisted. This was about the kids. If it was made to be about a sick coach, what would they do when he was gone? They needed to learn what was possible if they would only give their best effort and come together as a band of brothers.

Still, that impulse of "doing this for Coach" was inescapable. The players loved Jeremy, and they had this season, these ten-plus games, to show how they felt. They wanted an excuse to win big anyway. The previous season, 8–2 before play-offs, had given them a taste. Again, they'd turned the program around, doubling the previous season's win total. But in the first round of the play-offs, Emanuel County Institute had drubbed them 51–8.

The Patriots had had a long winter to think about what separated them from the team that had dispatched them so easily. It also helped that Greenville would have fifteen starters returning for 2009. There was great size along the offensive line and lightning speed in the backfield. If Greenville football was going to make a statement, the time was now. The potential was present. Jeremy's ALS brought an additional poignancy to the situation. The players got behind their goal, and the town got behind the players.

A team is composed of diverse individuals who share a moment of time and a common goal. The team has only that moment. The next year the older guys will be gone, the younger ones will replace them, and the dynamic and the feel won't be quite the same. The challenges, the schedule, the world, will all be a little different. It will be a different team with its own moment.

A team comes together and says, "Here we are. There are many different personalities among us; taken separately, we are more different than similar. Our gifts vary. Our futures will take us in many unknown directions and separate many of us over time. But today we are here, today we're together, and we're fused together by our dedication to carve out a legacy.

"Someday our paths may cross again—maybe at a reunion, maybe by mere chance in some distant place, when two of us meet on the highway of life. At that time we'll either celebrate what we do today or we'll smile ruefully in the shared understanding of what might have been, what is no longer possible.

"What remains is *now*—this one moment in time, this goal we seek, these talents God has given us. What will we make of *now*?"

Nobody on the team may articulate it exactly that way.

Nobody may fully grasp what it is that they feel about this team. But someday, they'll all understand:

Our moment together was special.

It did not happen by chance.

It was not like anyone else's moment.

It was ours, and within it—anything was possible.

The Sum of the Parts

The 2009 Greenville Patriots were a complex machine powered by many interconnected cogs. Each brought unique qualities to the gridiron. Each was determined to make his coach proud. They included (to name just a few):

The Prospect: Kenarious Gates

Kenarious was the big guy who was going places. He would play college ball, and it would probably be in Division I. At six-foot-four inches and three hundred pounds, he had the size to plug a hole even in big-time college football. He anchored a dominating veteran Greenville line, and he commanded visits from recruiters from all the regional universities that fielded teams.

But if Kenarious was a giant, he wasn't the angry type. He led quietly, but he led with heart. He was also a top student, which only helped his image among the college scouts. By the beginning of the season, Vanderbilt had already offered him a scholarship. So had Mississippi State, Kentucky, and a couple of teams from the Atlantic Coast Conference. But his dream was to play for the University of Georgia Bulldogs, who hadn't yet made him an offer. So Kenarious chose to focus on his team goals and his dedication to Jeremy Williams, his mentor and his hero.

The Athlete: Kentavious Caldwell-Pope

Kentavious's future was in another sport, basketball. He was destined to be the state's top player in that sport, to make every all-American team, including the prestigious McDonald's All-American squad, to be rated as the nation's third best shooting guard—and he would sign a basketball scholarship to play for Georgia. There were whispers that after a year of college, he could be in the NBA.

At Greenville, though, Kentavious was simply too good an athlete not to use on a football field, so he was plugged in at wide receiver.

The Speed Merchant: Mario Alford

Mario was another crossover athlete, his sport being track and field. He was the state champion in the one hundred meters. The punch line was that he had developed his skills at a school without a track. Greenville simply didn't have the facilities, so he trained in the tall, unkempt off-season grass of the football practice field. When the grass got to be knee-high, Mario would train on the hot asphalt of the parking lot. Then he would go to meets and outrun elite sprinters from schools that had expensive, all-weather tracks.

College recruiters could see Mario Alford as a receiver or perhaps a defensive back, where his blinding speed guaranteed that he would never be run down. But Greenville used him at quarterback, because that was the need. It was the one missing piece on the team, and since the Patriots ran a spread attack, Mario could be deadly at running option plays.

THE INSPIRATION: RICKEY BELL

As a defensive end, Rickey's job was to rush the passer. But Jeremy Williams had seen him rushing in the wrong direction. Rickey had led a tough life, losing both his parents when he was very young. He'd been raised by a grandmother and needed a mentor, a father figure.

Attending Greenville High and playing for the Patriots represented Rickey's chance to turn things around. Jeremy Williams had taken him under his wing, and so had Rickey's teammates. He didn't know much about football in the beginning, but what he saw was a group of young men like himself and a head coach who fit his picture of everything a father should be. Coach G, the chaplain, spent time with him, as did Tripp Busby and the other coaches.

All these people had a message for Rickey: You are somebody. God loves you. You have gifts and talents and a chance for a great life. All you have to do is show up, do the work, and make the right choices.

They showed him how to be respectful, how to dress neatly, how to hang in there when life pushed back. They also showed him how to fight off blockers and get to the quarterback, and he became an on-field terror as well as an off-the-field good citizen.

At Greenville High, Rickey Bell found a family. It even included Brenda Hudson, the school principal, who told Michael Carvell of the *Atlanta Journal-Constitution* that Rickey was one of her favorite students. He was, in short, an inspiration—one among many. And this particular inspiration beat the odds that were stacked against him and graduated.

ALL IN THE FAMILY

Vincent Warner was a player who had turned his life around in 2007. He took it personally when his suspension, early in that season, directly contributed to a key one-point loss. Coach Williams was upset with him, of course, but never turned him away, never wrote Vincent off.

Instead, the head coach showed him that life wasn't just about football. It was about the kind of person he was becoming, the kind of family member. The suspension was an opportunity to take adversity and make something positive out of it. It could be a growth experience. And it was.

Vincent's father had passed away the year before. Now, on an occasion when Jeremy was discouraged, he received a text from Vincent: "Keep your head up, Dad."

That text meant the world to Jeremy. It symbolized for him the best of his mission as a coach for teenage boys. And it was just one little example of something wonderful that was happening in Greenville, Georgia, as the 2009 football season drew near.

During a time when Jeremy's physical body was beginning to fail, the body of support from the community was becoming stronger than ever—the players, the other coaches, the parents, the faculty, the churches. They never let him forget that he and his family were not alone.

The days of Hardee's bacon cheeseburgers were over. Now the churches in the community took turns serving the team their pregame dinner. Players gathered in fellowship halls and church kitchens while deacons and church members cooked for them, doling out heaping servings of carbs and loving affirmation, promising they'd be there to cheer from the stands.

Members of the community and the other coaches looked for ways to support Jeremy as they saw him struggle with the physical demands of coaching. He could no longer shout during practices and games—his pipes just weren't up to the job—so the other coaches spoke more. They also handled washing the clothes, getting ice, lining off the field, etc. At halftime and before games, Tripp Busby and the other coaches would talk to the team, then respectfully give the floor to Jeremy to say a few key words. (Jeremy also learned to use body language and facial expressions to get across his message, often a glare that communicated, "Don't do that again!")

The community and coaches also stepped up to help with Jeremy's growing mobility problems. The practice field was at the bottom of a steep hill, and the assistant coaches and players noticed that it took a great deal of Jeremy's strength to climb it each day returning to the field house. Word got out, and within forty-eight hours the funds had been raised for a golf cart.

Zeke Parks, president of the Greenville High School Touchdown Club, called Jennifer to give her the news. He said, "Some folks here in Meriwether County wanted Coach Williams to have a cart so he could get around the grounds and practice field a little easier. We want his energies to go into coaching and mentoring rather than climbing or walking."

Jennifer whooped. "That's wonderful! Thank you—and we want to know everyone who contributed, so we can express our gratitude to them."

"They don't want any credit," laughed Zeke. "This is just something they wanted to do out of their love and support for your husband. But we do have one request: We want you to drive the cart onto the field during practice so we can give it to him—you and the kids, of course."

"Oh, but Zeke, I don't know about that part! Jeremy can't stand to have practice interrupted."

"Just leave that to me. We'll do it toward the end of practice, and you won't get into any trouble."

That's exactly what happened. Jennifer and the kids drove the little red golf cart onto the practice field while the team, the coaches, and members of the community applauded. Jeremy could only laugh and shake his head.

And then, a little later, came the phone. School and system administrators were concerned about Jeremy's ability to communicate and wanted to help. Because of their dedication, he received one of the first touch-screen phones in Meriwether County—far easier for him to handle than a phone requiring him to deal with keys and buttons.

In so many ways, the community was strong and generous for a man who had been strong and generous for them. Around Greenville, it was clear to everyone that football was only the smallest part of what mattered in life; it was just one more vehicle to allow people to minister to one another. These efforts were about community, about character, about family coming together.

Not that football didn't have a role to play.

From September through November, as a matter of fact, the game was going to take center stage. And though he could still walk, still speak and plan and coach, who could say whether this might be Jeremy's final season?

One thing was for certain: it was going to be a special season. Jeremy knew it. The town knew it. The players knew it too. They were ready.

THE SEASON OF A LIFETIME

The 2009 season began with a home game against Manchester High, the school down the road where Jeremy had begun his coaching career. For many years, Manchester had dominated its local rival, but the series had recently grown more competitive. It had become the annual season opener, and Meriwether County folks looked forward to it all summer.

Opening games can be sloppy as players knock away the off-season rust. Defenses are typically ahead of offenses, which tend to be slightly out of sync. This game was no exception. But Greenville won it 14–7, a come-from-behind victory in the closing minute of the game.

No one could have expected the offensive outpourings that followed from the Patriots in coming weeks. The spread attack came together as a well-oiled machine. Greenville won a road game against the Walnut Grove Warriors, 33–20, then a close in-region game against Columbus's Brookstone Cougars the following week, 27–25.

Greenville was 3–0 at that point but still unranked in the *Atlanta Journal-Constitution*'s poll for Class A football. It was after a dominating 56–0 victory over Schley County in week four that Greenville first entered the rankings at number ten.

But were the 2009 Patriots for real? They'd know the following week, when they traveled to undefeated number-five-ranked Chattahoochee County for a huge regional showdown. Greenville won the game by 20 points.

By now it was clear that big things were possible for this team. The Patriots were building confidence. They were in the middle of the regional slate, their offense was powerful, and their defense was beginning to pitch shutouts—they'd have an incredible six of them over an eight-game period. The team began to climb through the top-ten rankings. The stands were filling up for home games, and the team that had been 4–6 a couple of years ago was now a juggernaut, the talk of middle Georgia.

But what about elsewhere? In Atlanta, Georgia Tech was putting together an ACC championship season. The Georgia Bulldogs were weaker than usual. The Atlanta Falcons were fairly mediocre. The state was in the early grip of a terrible recession, just like the rest of the world. Good news seemed at a premium—and what the Patriots were doing was definitely good news. Toward the end of the season, when the Patriots were 10–0 and headed for the playoffs, their story went viral, largely through a series of articles written by Michael Carvell and Steve Hummer of the *Atlanta Journal-Constitution*. In time, people everywhere were discussing the story of Jeremy Williams, his family, his team.

Jeremy and Jennifer talked quietly in the evenings about the amazing trajectory of the story they had lived. They could see that God was using their experiences to encourage other people—even people all across the nation they might never meet. Their faith and courage were refreshed by the evidence that Romans 8:28 was really true: "And we know that in all things God works together for the good of those who love him, who have been called according to his purpose." More and more, they were understanding that nothing in life is meaningless. That God can and does use anything—even the most painful circumstances—for his glory and for the benefit of his children.

It was great to be 10–0 from a professional standpoint, a football standpoint. But Jeremy and Jennifer believed with all their hearts that something much greater than that was transpiring—something that served God's kingdom.

The dream was to get to the Georgia Dome in downtown Atlanta and play on television for the Georgia state Class-A championship.

The Patriots didn't quite get there. In the second round of the play-offs, they ran into Wilcox County, a team that had recently become powerful and would ultimately become the state champions. A few possessions into the Wilcox County game, Greenville was down 27–0. The team was in shock at halftime, but their motto was, "We never quit." The Patriots outscored their opponent for the rest of the game but could never quite catch up.

The Williamses were heartbroken—but only for a day or two. If football had been the center of their universe, the loss would have been a bitter pill. But they knew by this time that God was at work and that he hadn't written the last word yet. Jeremy hugged his players and thanked them for the incredible effort they had put forth all season.

The brief moment of the 2009 Patriots was over. Many would return for 2010—including Jeremy—but others would depart. Kenarious Gates would play the position of offensive lineman at the University of Georgia, just as he dreamed. Vincent Warner would play for West Georgia, and Mario Alford would play wide receiver at Georgia Military. All three players earned scholarships. The other seniors would move on to the next chapters in their lives, the underclassmen would step into their places, and new freshmen would arrive to fill out the team. Now it was time for the drudgery of off-season training.

But not a player in that locker room would forget this season of a lifetime. Together they had achieved something, and the memory of it would be their bond.

18

THREE WISE MEN

VERY FEW THINGS HAPPEN IN THIS WORLD WITHOUT THE contributions of many diverse hands. When the story is written, we often forget their names—if their names were ever known in the first place.

If the story of Jeremy and Jennifer Williams has traveled far and wide, it was helped along by a series of individuals who used their own gifts and talents to increase the reach of the events that happened in a small town, in a quiet corner of the Southern world.

Jeremy and Jennifer don't believe such things happen by chance. They attest that God has overarching purposes for everything that occurs, whether momentous or minuscule. They believe he uses people even when those people don't realize it. All of us, as a matter of fact, play our roles in a vast story whose ultimate meaning we will only see in another life.

Before the events of this chapter ever occurred, the Williamses believed God would use their story in the interest of his kingdom, his deep and redeeming love for humanity. So when three men—three wise and gifted men—stepped forward to assist the story on its journey, Jeremy and Jennifer could not be surprised.

By this time, they were well attuned to the spiritual nuances of their lives. They knew God was on the move, and it was only a matter of waiting to see when and how he would take hold of the story and share it with the world.

These three men, of course, were not the only agents of promotion. Many other quiet voices and faithful servants made their own contributions. Some of them can be detected on the periphery of the story: a coaching friend of Jeremy's, a listening ear at the National High School Coaching Association, a grateful parent writing comments on a website.

But these three are good representatives. They helped the story along simply by being willing, in Jeremy's words, to "do what they do." One wrote for a newspaper. One made films. One worked the business network.

Here are their stories.

The Journalist

Michael Carvell was a sportswriter for the *Atlanta Journal-Constitution*. During a time of transition in the newspaper industry, his beat was a relatively new one: college recruiting. It came about largely due to the obsessive fan interest over which universities would land top high school talent.

Carvell often dealt with surprisingly explosive material. The actual football season may last only three months, but recruiting fever is never out of season. And when he reported that any particular blue-chip recruit was going to a particular school, he was immediately an object of wrath for the fans of that school's rivals. Anxious fans were prone to kill—or at least harass—the messenger. This stuff was volatile.

Michael sought to supplement his reporting with solid features from the high school sports world. There were hundreds of schools in Georgia, nearly all of them with athletic programs and many of them, Michael assumed, with stories of at least some human interest.

So Michael put out the word that he was hoping to find a really good high school football story. He reached out through e-mail to coaches across the state; he got on the phone and called the usual suspects. "Looking for a strong personal story," he told them. "Maybe even something that could sustain a series of articles." A series, of course, sells more than one paper. It promotes regular reading, and that's vital in the struggling newspaper realm.

Michael heard from coaches far and wide. Many of them wanted him to write about, say, the local quarterback who had ratcheted up his studies and cut down on his interceptions. Others wanted him to do an in-depth article about the new defensive alignment they were installing. Coaches love positive publicity for their programs. There were many well-meaning suggestions, but not too many keepers.

Then there was an e-mail from a high school coach in Heard County, Georgia—Michael no longer remembers which one. This coach said he had a friend who was having a big season with a small school—Greenville High in Meriwether County. But the selling point was this: The coach was suffering from a terminal illness. He also had a little boy who was confined to a wheelchair due to a birth defect. And the whole town, the whole school, really the whole community had risen up to cheer on this coach to a state championship before he died.

Michael read the e-mail twice. *That*, he thought, *is a story.*

Soon he was en route to Greenville to check out the details. What he saw and experienced was a wonderful vignette from small-town America, but also a universal parable of courage and spiritual faith. This was so much more enriching than writing about which college Johnny Hotshot was changing his commitment to this week. Readers needed to see what Jeremy Williams was all about. They needed to meet his charismatic little boy and his steel magnolia of a wife and, of course, the little girl who tied the coach's shoelaces every morning. It was a wholesome and heartbreaking saga, played out under Friday night lights.

The first installment of Michael's "Season of a Lifetime" series appeared on November 13, 2009. Its two thousand words introduced readers to the coach, his family, his team, and his challenge. Through the season of Thanksgiving and the beginning of Christmastime, the stories continued to appear—reports of the Patriots' progress, an exploration of ALS, and other angles. Columnist Steve Hummer contributed an article as well, a profile of Jennifer, and the series created a buzz in cyberspace.

The Internet may have stolen circulation from most papers, but it has also opened up readership as articles are forwarded, shared through social media, and linked. Carvell's excellent series was the one force, apart from God's hand, that caused Jeremy's story to break wide open nationally. ESPN took an interest. So did HBO.

But two other men did more than listen.

They got busy.

The Filmmaker

Rick Cohen knew something about football. He had played Ivy League college ball, for the Pennsylvania Quakers, during the early eighties. But he would build his career in film, forming an Atlanta production company called Endorphin Entertainment. His documentary *Faded Glory* told the story of a band of aging amateur baseball players holding on to their dreams in the midst of life crises. *And the Lord Said . . . Smack 'Em in the Mouth* was a frank examination of the intersection of football violence and Christian spirituality.

One Sunday morning, Rick's business partner called to ask if he'd read the Atlanta sports page. There was a story there, he insisted, that had Endorphin written all over it.

Rick read the article and was fascinated. It wasn't the best timing, unfortunately; he was caught up in distribution negotiations for his recent films. But he had to admit that the Jeremy Williams story perfectly fused the themes he had already explored.

The problem, of course, was that the Cinderella season was largely history. He couldn't film events that had already happened. He also worried that larger, richer filmmakers would edge him out. Still, he and his partner couldn't stop thinking about this story.

The two of them drove to Greenville to meet with Jeremy in his office. Rick pointed out that HBO, ESPN, and the other "heavy hitters" might have had impressive names, but they hadn't bothered to drive down to Meriwether County the way the Endorphin duo had. *We're here,* was their message. *We care.*

Jeremy liked the idea, but he wanted to pray about it with his wife.

Fair enough. Rick returned to Atlanta. He didn't hear from Jeremy for forty days

Then, just about the time he'd decided his chances were gone, Rick got the phone call. Jeremy's family had been chosen by *Extreme Makeover: Home Edition* to receive a new home. Jeremy had been in Colorado, involved with filming, and then he had gotten ill—seriously ill. But he had prayed about this film venture, and the answer was yes.

It was an interesting project. Rick was a Jewish filmmaker telling a Christian story. But he graciously allowed Jeremy and Jennifer to tell it their way, and he made a moving film called *Season of a Lifetime* that documented not the 2009 season but the one that would mark Jeremy's final year of coaching—2010. Released in 2012, the film brought tears to the eyes of audiences in churches and auditoriums across the nation. It seemed destined for viewing (and changing lives) in locker rooms and home Bible study groups and everywhere the medium of film could travel.

The football footage was thrilling, clearly filmed by someone who knew and cared about the game. The coaches, players, and people of Greenville had a chance to speak for the cameras. But the highlights of the documentary were the glimpses of family life at the Williams home—scenes such as Jeremy, in his wheelchair, helping his little son out of his own chair and into the bed. It was impossible to watch something like that and not be profoundly moved by the quiet courage of the Williams family, strengthened by love and faith in the midst of so much sadness.

The documentary showed visually what the newspaper had described in prose, and the Williams story continued to spread.

THE BUSINESSMAN

Andy Robinson was an executive with Aflac Insurance in Columbus, Georgia. He intimately knew the city that had produced Jeremy and Jennifer Williams, but he hadn't heard their story until he, too, picked up an Atlanta newspaper during November 2009.

Andy was so inspired by Michael Carvell's account that he began passing it on to friends. He was dating a woman with the serious disease of lupus, so the courage of the Williams family resonated with him. And he found he couldn't just put the paper away and forget about what he had read. He had to see this coach with his own eyes.

Andy found himself climbing into his car to drive the fifty miles to Greenville and see the Patriots take on Wilcox County. He sat in the stands and looked around at the crowd—good country people united by their passion for the high school team. And it was clear how they felt about the man who shambled up and down the sidelines, headphones affixed to his ears, grabbing shoulder pads and yelling instructions into the ear holes of helmets.

In some ways, it wasn't the best game for Andy to attend—or maybe it was, for the same reasons. It was the first game of the season the Patriots had lost. Wilcox County jumped out to that huge first-quarter lead and killed the Greenville dream of a state championship.

But Andy then watched as the whole team went to the center of the field for prayer at the end. He was moved by the maturity of the heartbroken players, who had wanted so badly to win for their coach. Parents came and huddled with the team—local fans, too, then Wilcox players and coaches. It was everything competitive sports should be about, yet so seldom was.

Again some invisible magnetic force pulled Andy forward, and he was on the field, wanting to say something to Jeremy Williams, to express the admiration he felt.

He recognized Columbus columnists, an Atlanta sportswriter, and then: "Andy!"

He looked up, startled at the sound of his name, and there was his brother Pete, an Atlanta attorney. The two hadn't seen each other for some time. But both Robinsons had felt their hearts tugged to this place. They caught up a little as the festivities slowly came to an end and Jeremy said a few words to his team before motoring away on his golf cart.

A little later, Andy stood in the background and listened to Jeremy give an interview to a sportswriter. The words were slurred, the speaker was tired, the biggest game of a lifetime had been lost, yet Jeremy's warrior spirit prevailed. He praised his players, his coaches, his fans, his God.

Jeremy never knew or noticed the insurance man who stood quietly in the shadows, listening so intently to that interview. But that man made a quiet commitment to help the world hear the coach's story. Tears flowed on the drive home as he thought about the lessons of the evening and wondered what to do next.

What he wanted, he decided, was to see Jeremy Williams acclaimed as the national high school coach of the year.

He didn't know what that involved. He had no connections in the world of high school sports, but he was pretty sure that other coaches were going to win state championships and be nominated. Other coaches would have bigger, flashier teams in Texas or Florida or California and be better connected politically. But Jeremy was going to win that award, and Andy Robinson would see to it.

At home in Columbus, Andy began researching the National

High School Coaching Association (NHSCA), how it accepted nominations, and what the process entailed. But he fought his war on other fronts too. In December the *Atlanta Journal-Constitution* asked for nominations for the sports story of the year, and Jeremy's series was listed. So Andy mounted a campaign to get all his friends and all their friends to vote for it. This, of course, would bring the series another cycle of attention from readers.

When the story of the year solicitation appeared, the comment section was filled with inspiring stories and testimonies from former players, their parents, coaches, fans, and readers who had been inspired and encouraged by Carvell's series. Georgia Tech had won a conference championship and gone to a bowl game. Tiger Woods had endured a scandal. Big-time sports rocked on as usual. But for *Journal-Constitution* readers there was no contest. They chose the story that touched their hearts.

But Andy was still seeking out other ways to publicize the story of Jeremy Williams and Greenville High. He contacted the University of Memphis public relations department, the ALS Association, anyone who might take an interest in the story. Then he approached the NHSCA itself.

The organization is located in Pennsylvania, Andy had discovered. He discovered the names of Rob Sherrill, who chaired the selection committee for awards, and Bob Ferraro Sr., the founder and CEO, and began corresponding with both.

Andy is a humble, quiet, and unassuming man who tends to avoid the limelight, but he's nothing if not persistent. Over six months, NHSCA officials received reams of information on Jeremy Williams and his work. And in June 2010, just after the airing of *Extreme Makeover*, Jeremy Williams was indeed proclaimed the national high school coach of the year.

Once that happened, Andy Robinson felt that his work had been accomplished, so he faded into the background. For a long time Jeremy knew nothing about all the work that the insurance executive had done on his behalf. Only when the NHSCA asked Andy to contact Jeremy to discuss details did Jeremy and Jennifer finally discover there was a man named Andy Robinson, a messenger angel of the Internet, phone lines, and the US mail. They quickly became good friends.

Meanwhile, Andy's seeds began to sprout in other places. The Memphis Tigers named a spring football award after Jeremy, and the NHSCA plans to establish an annual courage award in Jeremy's honor.

Andy may hide his own light under a bushel, but he has amped up Jeremy's light by megawatts, that Christ might shine before the whole world.

19

EXTREME HOME MIRACLES

WHEN PEOPLE SHARED THE WILLIAMS STORY, IT WAS EASY to overlook Josie.

The story, of course, started with the courageous coach who soldiered on while a debilitating disease took increasing control over his body. Then there was the strong and supportive wife by his side—everyone who visited Meriwether County came away impressed by the powerful marriage factor of the story. And Jacob, the charismatic little boy with spina bifida, seemed to complete the tableau.

Except that it didn't. There was a healthy, bright little girl in that picture, too, and she was integral to everything. She dutifully cared for her little brother, taking up for him at school and helping him at home. When she and Jacob were small, there had been an incident in a doctor's waiting room that demonstrated her spirit. A rambunctious little boy was creating havoc while his mother simply ignored him. At one point, he pulled Jacob's hair, and Jacob began to wail—but only for a second. By the time Jennifer could leap from her chair, Josie had that little boy pinned against the wall. *Nobody* fooled with her little brother!

Josie also helped care for her father and was obedient to her mother. She was an important part of God's provision for the Williams family. Jennifer couldn't have handled such a home without a cheerful, cooperative daughter by her side.

And looking back, Jennifer felt that God had made special provisions for Josie as well. It was a little touch that had God's fingerprints all over it, like so many things that happened in that crazy time between Jeremy's diagnosis and the home makeover.

Interestingly, Josie's teacher had the same observation. After the Colorado trip and the rest of the filming, the two Williams kids returned to school as celebrities. First- through third-graders lined up in the halls to give the returning stars a rousing welcome. Josie's teacher wondered how a third-grade girl would handle such special treatment. Yet when the time came, Josie went straight to her seat, sat down, and went to work as if nothing were changed.

Later, her teacher said to Jennifer, "I knew what your family was going through when I got your daughter in my class. I thought maybe God was sending me to minister to her. But as the year has gone on, I think it's been just the opposite. God sent Josie to bless me."

Like her mother, Josie adored animals—animals of every kind, though horses were her favorite. During the trying time when Jeremy and Jennifer got their bad news about his health, a menagerie of three dogs and two cats added to the chaos of the household. The family wouldn't have had it any other way, but five domestic animals inside the tiny house were plenty.

Then Patriot came into their lives.

One day, Jennifer and Jacob were pulling into the driveway

in the truck when they witnessed a fur-flying ruckus in the back-yard. The three dogs had cornered some animal and were going after it pretty good. Jennifer hurried from the truck, clapping her hands and calling off the hounds. They turned obediently and began trotting in her direction, leaving behind them a little gray ball of fur seemingly no worse for the wear.

Jennifer thought it had to be a rabbit. It turned out to be a kitten—a gray tabby kitten. But why didn't the kitten show the results of the attack? And why did it trot right behind its attackers rather than scamper to safety in the trees?

Later in the day, Jennifer drove up again after picking up Josie from school. This time the kitten was sitting on the front porch. Josie jumped out of the truck as the kitten came right up to the vehicle's door.

Josie immediately picked up the little animal, which purred in her arms.

"Darling, you know what your dad is going to say," Jennifer sighed. "We can't take in another animal."

Josie knew that, but she was in love with this kitten anyway. She played with it until her father came home. Jeremy looked at the furry newcomer, then at his daughter, and seemed to understand the kitten was special. "What will we name it?" he asked, "Tiger or Patriot?" Those were the family's favorite school mascots.

"*Patriot!*" shouted Josie. Patriot let out a pleased meow, and from that day onward, during the tough times the family experienced, Josie had a special friend to give her joy and attention. No matter who fed Patriot, he only had eyes for the little girl.

One day, a couple of years later, Jennifer was walking to the barn to do her chores when she realized she was being watched. Patriot sat on a fence post, calmly regarding her. There was something strange about this cat—she was sure of it—something about the knowing look in the eyes that met hers. "Patriot," she said, "you're here for my daughter, aren't you? With all we're going through, you came to show God's love to Josie."

The cat hopped down off the fence and sauntered into the underbrush. Jennifer later said, "He looked like he had angel wings."

Josie thought that was pretty cool; Jeremy's response was, "You've been reading too many Frank Peretti novels."

Might have been just an overactive imagination. But that cat was with the family right up to the very week before the *Extreme Makeover* crew came around. Then the cat was gone. His work, Jennifer thought, was done.

TELL US ABOUT YOURSELF

So the time came for *Extreme Makeover: Home Edition*. The persistence of the play-group mothers—and Jennifer's confirmed prayer—finally convinced Jeremy and Jennifer to apply for the show and a new home.

At one point, the Williamses had to give detailed information about each member of the family.

Josie's form was the first to be completed. It required three hours of work, and gave a good picture of Josie's love of horses, what TV shows she liked, and so on. Jennifer sat at the kitchen table and entered her information into the computer.

One of the things Josie mentioned on her form was a tree house. She'd been after her dad to build her a pink one, and there simply hadn't been enough time or energy. Jennifer smiled at that entry. If they won the makeover, she knew that many things would be done for Jeremy and for Jacob, who had physical disabilities. Again, Jennifer realized how easily people who didn't know Josie could overlook her. So she prayed, *Lord, if it's your will for us to receive a makeover, please let there be something very special for Josie—just for her.*

Jennifer completed Josie's form and then prayed about what to do with it. *Lord, should I go on and e-mail Josie's information now or wait until I've finished all of them?* Jennifer felt God's confirmation and went ahead and e-mailed Josie's form by itself.

While filling out her own form, Jennifer had to tell what she enjoyed in her free time. She wrote, "A bubble bath—ha ha!" As if she ever had time for bubble baths. But then, as she typed, she suddenly was reminded about one of her favorite things: claw-foot tubs. She had adored them ever since she was a little girl.

Her hands hovered over the keys.

Lord, if the makeover is part of your plan—and I walk into our bathroom and find a claw-foot tub—I'll know that is your special gift just for me. A grand demonstration of your love for me.

When Jennifer was done, she e-mailed the other three forms and went on with her life.

The Old Rugged Cross

On that wonderful Sunday morning when the Williamses heard the knock on their door, the door wouldn't come open. It was habitually stuck and required some special convincing. The *Extreme Makeover* crew were left waiting for an extra moment or two, wondering where the family could be.

But that wasn't the first crisis of the morning. That came earlier, when Jennifer couldn't find her favorite cross necklace.

She had made it for herself while pregnant with Jacob as a visual token to remind her that Jesus was always with her. The necklace was long, with a black cord, and a cross crafted of metal that had come from a nearby Hobby Lobby store. She never went anywhere without that necklace. But now it had disappeared at a time when it was particularly important to her to wear it. If there were going to be TV cameras, she wanted to make sure she was seen with the cross of Jesus Christ. But that cross had vanished into thin air.

She had two other cross necklaces, both with less personal meaning and both shorter in length. One necklace was made of shredded paper and dipped in wax—an analogy of how life can tear us apart, but Jesus is the one who holds us together. The other necklace was made of pewter and black beads. Neither necklace was as special to her, but they would have to do. She put on the beaded necklace and waited to receive either a door knock or a phone call.

At the end of that week, when the Williamses returned home from Colorado and saw their lovely, handicap-accessible home, Jennifer was wearing a paper cross. The crew member who was adjusting her microphone said, "Oh, I don't think you can wear a necklace, Jennifer."

"Are you sure?"

"It will interfere with the mike and give us all kinds of sound problems."

"But this is important to me. Can we at least try it?"

"Sure—we'll give it a try. But I don't think it will work."

The filming went off without a hitch. If Jennifer had worn her favorite necklace, the metal cross would have hung beside the microphone causing interference. But the two shorter necklaces did just fine.

Jennifer said yet another silent prayer of gratitude to the God of details, who thinks of everything. Her beloved necklace would never have made the cut. It was too long. But because she had been forced to substitute with two shorter necklaces, people across the world would see she was a believer.

The next time Jennifer was with the play-group moms, she told them the story. Her friend Jennifer Vaughn, the same one who had been instrumental in starting the *Extreme Makeover* letter-writing campaign, now said, "You made a cross necklace for me that was just like yours, remember? I want you to wear it until yours turns up."

"Thank you, Jennifer. I'd love to!"

"And let me tell you something," said Jennifer V to Jennifer W. "When you find your own cross, it will be a special moment. It will be just the moment when you need it."

What a spiritually perceptive thought. Jennifer hoped her cross would turn up soon.

We're Here for Jeremy

The house, of course, was a marvel. The family had known it would be wonderful, but they couldn't have imagined *how* wonderful.

The *Extreme Makeover* folks were noted for their innovative designs, but they had gone all out on this one. For one thing, it was the first fully modular home the show had ever assembled. Built by Martinsville, Virginia's Nationwide Homes (a subsidiary of Palm Harbor Homes), twelve prebuilt sections were trucked in and set in place. Given that *Extreme Makeover* homes had to be built within a week, this allowed for more care and detail in the construction. The doors in the house worked by remote control so that Jeremy and Jacob could come and go easily. And, of course, there were plenty of attentive, personalized features throughout the home.

Needless to say, the community was enthusiastic about a big TV show coming to Pine Mountain Valley, and many wanted to help. In fact, far more volunteers turned up at the designated gathering spot than could be used. Waiting for shuttle buses to take them to the work site were Memphis teammates, past and current high school coaches and players, church friends, and family members—plus a number of people who didn't even know Jeremy and Jennifer but had traveled for hours to be part of the build.

One of those waiting was Larry Margarum, Jeremy's boyhood friend. Larry had served as best man at Jeremy and Jennifer's wedding. But Larry, a self-effacing individual, saw Jeremy as the best man he knew. Jeremy was his brother. His brother was in need. And Larry would do whatever he could to help.

Larry stood quietly in the teeming crowd, holding his toolbox. He realized that some of the crowd were there because they were attracted to the cameras and the bright lights. But Larry didn't care about any of that. He just wanted to get to work.

Jeremy's mother, standing by the coordinators, spotted Larry in the crowd. "That one there—he gets on the shuttle bus every day," she said. Not only was Larry a family friend but he was a cabinetmaker, the kind of wood worker who calls himself a craftsman though others call him an artist.

"What part did you work on?" someone would ask Larry later while he sat in the Williamses' new house. He scanned the room and pointed to a table. "I built this," he said. "And the picture frame over there? I built that too." He then led a little tour of the house and indicated that he had built some focal piece in every room.

It turned out that the designers and supervisors had recognized the quality of Larry's work right away. Before long, those in charge were bringing him special assignments. He'd been integral to the whole process.

But he didn't want to talk about it on TV.

When someone heard Larry talking about his work and brought over a camera for an interview, Larry refused to talk. "I don't do TV," he said. "I'm here for Jeremy and Jennifer and their kids."

By the end of the week, the show crew wanted to talk to Larry about working for them. "You need to sign on with us," they said. "We'll pay you a salary, and you travel with us and help get the houses built right."

"No thank you," said Larry. "I told you I don't do TV. I'm just here for my friends."

Larry had no illusions about himself. He was just a regular guy from Columbus who'd had his ups and downs and who appreciated his old friends from childhood. They were one of the beautiful things that had happened to him, and he had their backs forever, just as they had his. He'd been feeling helpless lately with all that was happening to Jeremy. But now, with this chance to help build a house for his buddy, he was feeling pretty good about life.

REVELATION

In makeover shows, the climactic segment is known as the reveal. The reveal of the Williamses' new home, when the bus moved and they saw where they would be living, was one of the most exciting moments of their lives. They could only laugh and weep a few tears as they walked through their transformed living space.

This truly was a miracle; it would change their everyday life just when the change meant so much. Jeremy no longer needed to deal with steps, the layout was open and just right for wheelchairs; and there were nifty little touches everywhere, such as displays of the couple's love letters in the bedroom. ("She wrote me a lot!" Jeremy laughed on the telecast; in truth, Jeremy had written the letters, not the other way around. Jennifer ribbed him about that more than once.)

The children's rooms—and the children's reactions—were filmed first. Jacob had a well-designed space in which everything was easy for him to reach. A combination TV and computer, cutting-edge technology, had a touch screen.

Jennifer didn't see her daughter's wonderful horse-and-barn-themed room until later. When she walked in, she began to cry.

"What are you crying about, Mom?" asked one of the designers.

"I asked God for something very special for Josie," said Jennifer between tears. "And look—her tree house."

"You know, it's funny you should mention that," said the designer. "We received Josie's information forms earlier than the others, and we saw that she liked tree houses. We had already started on a design, as we did for each of the finalist families. Your other three forms came in at the last minute. Only because Josie's came in earlier did we have the time to change our designs and give her that tree house in her room."

Another amazing moment came when Jennifer entered her new bedroom. Out of the corner of her eye, she saw the master bath—with a claw-foot tub. The TV crew was mystified as to why so many things made this woman cry. "Hey, Mom," they asked. "Why are you crying? It's just a tub!"

"It's a special tub," said Jennifer. "It's a very specific answer to my prayer. It's a message that God loves me very much."

"Okay," said the cameraman, a little puzzled.

But the TV crew did respect the family's spiritual focus and tried to include it into the house's design. In fact, one of their many nice touches was to buy a beautiful family Bible and engrave it for the Williamses. They also bought children's Bibles for Josie and for Jacob. And in this, too, God was in the details.

A few months earlier, Jennifer had gone to a Christian bookstore and bought Bibles for her two children. She hid them for Christmas and did such a good job of it that she couldn't find them later, no matter how hard she looked. Before leaving for Colorado she'd told one of the show assistants to please be on the lookout for the Bibles when packing away the family's possessions.

During the reveal, both children found engraved children's Bibles in their rooms—the exact editions she had bought. Not the same Bibles—those had never turned up. It just happened that *Extreme Makeover* had ordered the same ones she had chosen many months before. To Jennifer, it was just another one of those small reminders of God's detailed love and care.

But not all the miracles the family experienced during that time were of the small variety. The TV episode ended with the family being told that the mortgage on their property had been completely paid off. This had been known to occur on episodes of *Extreme Makeover*, but it was far from guaranteed. "If you win the makeover, your mortgage might be paid off," *Extreme Makeover* had told Jeremy and Jennifer, "but we have nothing to do with it. The builder and the community come to that decision on their own."

And they did. The Williamses learned that Nationwide Homes had gotten involved in fund-raising for their financial needs. The mortgage owed on the property was $47,000, and the company also wanted to buy a special-needs van for the family. So their goal had been $100,000. Buckets were handed around the community, and people would put a check, a dollar, or a handful of change in it. One little boy dumped his entire piggy bank into the bucket. In the end, the mortgage was indeed paid off, and a very gracious couple provided the van.

Josie, who always named the family pets and anyone else that needed christening, promptly dubbed the van EB—for "Extremely Blessed." EB could make friends with Jennifer's truck, TJ ("Trust Jesus").

Even after all that, there was more to reveal. CVS, the pharmacy chain, stepped in to pay off the family's medical debts. And Columbus State University made it known that Josie and Jacob would have full college scholarships waiting for them as soon as they finished high school. (Prior to Jacob's birth, Edgewood Baptist Church had set up the Jacob Fund. Members anonymously gave to it, and it helps pay the boy's many medical needs.)

There were too many blessings to take in at once. Jeremy and Jennifer felt light-headed over all the good things being done for them, and particularly by the love shown to them by their community.

It was quite a reveal—a revelation of God in so many details. The house may have been shiny and new, but it had divine fingerprints all over it. There had been so many months of anxiety, of grieving over future prospects. And now it seemed as if the Lord—and his many angels—had done a thousand things to overwhelm the Williams family with love and grace.

A WORD FROM OUR SPONSOR

What happens on the day after "happily ever after"?

Life becomes strangely ordinary again. The TV crews leave town. The newspaper articles stop appearing. And if you're the Williams family, you take that one day to cry tears of joy—and keep doing what you do.

Except that a few things are different.

Jeremy was determined to keep coaching until he absolutely couldn't do it. Before the 2011 season began, that day arrived. He had no strength, no mobility, no voice. So he found he had to step away graciously from the career he had loved.

Jennifer went to work as an assistive technology specialist for Meriwether County School System, where she provided assistive technology for special-needs children. It was the last direction she had expected to go, but it fit like a glove. It was the job she felt she was born to do. She wasn't teaching science anymore, but she found that she could interact with many different teachers and students and there were many possibilities for service.

Because Jennifer was the only person now working, she was concerned about being the primary provider for the family. She felt guilty for worrying about these things. God had taken care of their every need. When had he ever failed them? The Williams family had seen miracles. Even so, doubt was raising its ugly head.

One day she was out in the shed thinking about these things—and, yes, worrying a little bit about them. There were so many boxes to go through. Their possessions had been neatly packed away for them when they left for Colorado. Some of the contents needed to be put in their proper place in the house; others needed to be thrown away or taken to the church or local thrift shop. The bills and the boxes seemed overwhelming to her at this moment. *Lord,* she prayed, *you've always been good to us. But we have so many needs. Will you continue to help us?*

Just as those words pulsed through her mind, something gleamed in the corner of her eye—something peeking out of one of the boxes. She reached out, knowing exactly what she was going to find: her cross necklace. It was the one thing that had been missing all these months.

"And Jennifer. Let me tell you something. When you find your own cross, it will be a special moment. It will be just the moment when you need it."

Her friend's words flashed through her memory and brought a revelation: Jesus was right there. He was in the shed with her as she went through boxes. He was in the new house, even as he had been in the old one. He was with them in their fresh challenges, just as he'd been with them in the former ones.

How could she ever doubt him?

Quite a trick God had performed with that simple necklace. First, he had taken it away because it wouldn't have made the telecast. Then he had restored it when she needed assurance of his presence.

And that wasn't all. There was one more miracle to come.

After their *Extreme Makeover* episode aired, Jennifer and her mom were sorting through boxes in the garage when Jennifer came across a little birdhouse. It was beautifully handcrafted of tiny sticks. Jennifer held it, wiped a little dust off it, and smiled. She didn't know who it was for, but she felt that it was a special gift for someone. She set it carefully aside.

Jennifer was taking classes for her master's degree. During that summer semester, she sat beside a girl who seemed to really need a friend. They talked, and Jennifer learned the girl's father had terminal cancer. Jennifer felt as if she had been sent to that class just to encourage this one person who needed it. She shared a little about what her family had been through, particularly with Jeremy's illness, and about just how good God is.

They only met in that class on three occasions. On the second of these, the girl talked sadly about her father again, and for some reason she mentioned that he really loved birdhouses. Jennifer's heart skipped a beat when she heard that.

On their third meeting—the last time they saw each other— Jennifer told her friend, "I have something for your dad in my car." Her friend smiled and thanked her. After class, Jennifer went out and retrieved the birdhouse.

"Oh, Jennifer!" the other woman gasped. "My dad will just love this. It will give him a wonderful day."

Jennifer felt the joy of knowing that God had led her to the very person the birdhouse was meant for.

20

IN HIS GRIP

THE ANCIENTS, LACKING TOOLS OF PRECISION, TENDED TO measure things by the breadth of a hand. But whose hand? The pink palm of a baby, with its stubby fingers, is quite different from a man's rough, worn knuckles.

Left to ourselves, we measure life by our own changing standards. But what if we measure by the breadth of God's hand? It's the one and only standard set for time and eternity. As the psalmist wrote, "Show me, Lord, my life's end and the number of my days; let me know how fleeting my life is. You have made my days a mere handbreath; the span of my years is nothing before you. Everyone is but a breath, even those who seem secure" (Ps. 39:4–5). The point is our lives are fleeting, yet placed in God's hands, they have eternal value.

From the time that they learned about Jeremy's ALS, both Jeremy and Jennifer attempted to see the shadow of eternity in the short span of their days. Jeremy loved telling people that really, his situation was no different than anyone else's. None of us know where the end of the yardstick is. So shouldn't we all be seizing the moment? Certainly the Bible tells us so.

All the same, Jennifer insisted that every day must be cherished. Anything that could be enjoyed right now, particularly as a family, should not be left for tomorrow. Duties and tasks could always be carried over, but family time must be cherished in the now.

Jacob had no real memories of a time when his dad didn't share his physical disabilities. But Josie could remember when her father could get down on the floor, wrestle with her, tickle her, effortlessly whisk her from the floor to sit on his lap. He had taken her on a glorious hunting trip, a memory she treasured. Actually, she had gone on hunting trips with him even before that, when she was so small he carried her in his backpack.

Robert, Jeremy's brother, also treasured memories of hunting. Hunting and fishing and outdoor life had bonded the two of them ever since childhood. But when Robert learned of Jeremy's diagnosis, Robert saw the writing on the wall. How many more seasons could Jeremy tramp through the woods with him? Maybe two—maybe just one.

Suddenly there was an urgency about their hunts. And Robert vowed to get Jeremy out there in the woods as often as he could for as long as he could.

Robert, who worked as a firefighter, began to arrange his hours and his vacations so that he and Jeremy would be able to hunt during the various seasons. He also put the word out, pulled a few strings, and called in a few markers to arrange some truly special memories. People were eager to help when they heard Jeremy's story. There was a trip to South Dakota to hunt pheasants, for instance, and the two of them went deer hunting in Kansas.

On many of these trips, Jeremy insisted on driving. They'd be in the car eighteen hours, twenty hours, twenty-two, and Robert would get a little nervous. "C'mon, dude, pull over," he would say. "Let me have the wheel for a while. You've gotta be tired by now."

But Jeremy was stubborn. The time would come when he'd lack the strength in his arms to steer, in his legs to operate the brakes and accelerator. He was extracting every physical opportunity from every situation, appreciating the limbs he had always taken for granted. There would be plenty of time later to sleep, to rest, to sit still.

Not every hunting trip involved a long-distance trek, however. Robert periodically helped a friend with chores on a farm—backbreaking labor, but the trade-off was that Robert and his brother were allowed to do all the hunting they wanted on those acres of good forest. They hunted for deer meat, then they hunted for trophies. They also did a little dove hunting, something at which Jeremy had always excelled. But over time, as the ALS progressed, his arms and hands grew weaker and less responsive, and he had to carry smaller guns.

Still, Robert wanted Jeremy to have the best possible outings and to see the country at the same time. So he began thinking about a new possibility.

Jeremy had always loved hunting wild turkeys. What if he could climax a lifetime of hunting with a wild-turkey grand slam?

Slammin'

The grand slam idea lit up Robert's imagination. It would involve thousands of miles of travel, and realistically, it had to be done within one season or it would never be finished. For most hunters, even serious ones, a wild-turkey grand slam was the work of five years of hunting, maybe twenty. That was no option for Jeremy.

The American grand slam is earned by shooting one mature, long-bearded tom turkey from each of the four main subspecies: Eastern, Osceola, Merriam's, and Rio Grande. They could be killed with shotgun or bow. The Eastern turkeys are wide ranging and perhaps the most common. Osceola is a Florida turkey. The Merriam's is a Rocky Mountains bird, and the Rio Grande is hunted in Texas, Oklahoma, or Kansas.

Until Robert began planning their trips together, Jeremy had never hunted out West. It was the kind of thing that his hectic coaching slate simply hadn't allowed. Robert had enjoyed taking him to Kansas and South Dakota and Tennessee, and now he reveled in making new adventures possible, though they both could see Jeremy's hands failing and his strength steadily ebbing. He would wait at one end of the field, and his friends would drive the birds in his direction. There would usually be some comical arguments about when to call the bird, when to wait, and so forth.

Jeremy and Robert had always been comfortable around each other. Now, they reveled in the chance to spend more time together than they had in years. The older brother watched the younger one, always the great athlete, dealing with the loss of his physical capacities, yet living in joy with the power of his God-given faith.

Jeremy had never been insistent or argumentative about his beliefs when the two of them were together. But now more than ever, Robert was astonished at the grace that shone from his brother's soul. As had happened with Chip, Robert did some soul searching of his own.

One day Robert looked at his brother struggling up another hill, and he thought, "This is it. This is the last hunt." And he began to cry, despite all his efforts at restraint. It was an unwritten rule among the brothers—as with so many men of the South—that they never cried in front of each other.

Jeremy looked up at him and said, "Don't you cry."

The two of them might have been kids again, one of them fallen from a bike. *Big boys don't cry.* It might have been Robert toughening up his little brother after Jeremy got hit by a pitch in backyard baseball. *Come on, now—be tough. Be a man.*

But they weren't kids anymore. This was life and death. "I'm going to cry," said Robert. "Okay?"

Jeremy patted his shoulder, and the two of them just stood for a second, feeling the breeze and listening to the birds and considering the future.

With the help of a relentless brother, Realtree Outdoors, and Chris Kirksey, Jeremy got his grand slam—and he did it within two months, something of a minor miracle. Realtree Outdoors' TV cameras followed every leg of the trip for a hunting show that would be broadcast on ESPN 2.

The story of Jeremy Williams just wouldn't stay home. It reached out yet again, inspiring another audience of viewers who could only respond by thinking, *Show me, Lord, my life's end and the number of my days; let me know how fleeting my life is.*

Redeeming the Time

As the hunting days came to a conclusion, then the days of coaching, then the days of standing and walking, Jeremy and Jennifer had to find new ways to think about what remained of their life together. Each month, sometimes each day, seemed to bring new decisions as Jeremy's illness progressed.

One day Jennifer was at the bookstore and picked up *A Lifetime of Wisdom. Embracing the Way God Heals You* by Joni Eareckson Tada, an author she admired. Years ago, as an athletic teenager, Joni was paralyzed from the neck down in a diving accident. She has an important ministry to the disabled, so Jennifer opened the pages eagerly. She flipped through the pages to a passage in which Joni speaks to a woman with a motor neuron disease who is contemplating whether to get a tracheotomy.

As it happened, Jeremy and Jennifer would be wrestling with this very decision in the near future. A tracheotomy is a permanent incision in the front of the throat. Having this procedure done would help Jeremy's breathing, but it would mean the end of his speaking. So a lot of prayer and soul-searching was going on.

In the book, Joni shares a verse from the New Testament: "But do not forget this one thing, dear friends: With the Lord a day is like a thousand years, and a thousand years are like a day" (2 Peter 3:8). The idea was not to measure time by the breadth of our own hands, but by God's. A mere moment is like all of time for him, and all of time like a mere moment. God doesn't live within time, as we do. He created it; he sees it from the outside. Time is like the gridiron of a football field, with its clear boundaries, and God sits in the skybox and sees beginning and end in one sweeping view.

Jennifer spent time thinking about this concept and then talked about it with Jeremy. What they decided was that if a moment of time can carry so much meaning for God—the value of a thousand years—then they should treat it the same way. Each moment of each day was filled with possibilities for God's kingdom. And only while he was in this life could Jeremy share the gospel with someone who needed it. Therefore they would do everything they could to fight the progression of the ALS and to give Jeremy meaningful time on this side of eternity—even if it meant his speaking voice was silenced. Jennifer had absolutely no complaints about that—anything that would keep Jeremy by her side was a winning proposition in her book.

The trach was a winner. It improved the quality of Jeremy's life exponentially. He had been breathing with a vent and a mask, and because he couldn't breathe and eat at the same time, tube feedings had become necessary. Now he would be able to lose the mask that covered his smile. In time, there was even the possibility of getting a Passy-Muir valve, which would allow Jeremy to speak with a trach.

Each moment is a unique gift from God, not to be repeated. It comes, it presents itself to us, and then it passes out of our grasp forever. As the Bible says, life is but a vapor that lingers briefly and is gone. This doesn't subtract from the significance of this life; on the contrary, it gives an urgency to every second. Paul wrote about how we must be "redeeming the time, because the days are evil" (Eph. 5:16 NKJV).

Jeremy and Jennifer Williams had committed themselves to redeeming whatever time they had left together, cherishing the gift of their minutes together, and continuing to live each moment for God's glory.

ON MESSAGE

Jeremy had led an active life from the time he was a toddler, and even with his retirement and the progressing ALS, he wasn't ready to stay at home all day, every day. And there were still things he could do. There were high school games to attend, where he would be surrounded by friends from the community, former players, and well-wishers of every kind. He could attend the "Run for Jeremy," a 5K run that benefited ALS research. He could even participate by riding in a wheelchair-accessible golf cart donated by Realtree Outdoors and driven by Jennifer's father. He could wheel himself outside on a lovely spring day and enjoy the country air.

But being the man he was, he also had to find a new way of coaching, a new way of doing what God had put him on the earth to do. And, of course, God was faithful in giving him the tools to do that.

God once asked Moses, "What is that in your hand?" (Ex. 4:2). He was referring to the staff that Moses carried, and the lesson was that any tool we might carry, no matter what it is, is also in the grip of God and can be used to do his work.

Jeremy didn't carry a staff, but what he found in his hand was his touch-screen phone, which gave him the ability to text.

Years ago, he had used his entire body to play football and glorify God. Even back then, he'd been a coach on the field, encouraging his teammates and modeling how a child of God handles every situation. In time, he had become a coach on the sidelines, using his mind and his voice and his overcoming spirit to exhort young people to reach their potential.

Now, it had all come down to a thumb. His arms no longer held much strength, but he could still tap out short messages. And one day he realized he could tap them out to more than one person at a time.

That was an aha moment.

On a practice field, Jeremy used to call on the team and coaches to circle around him and take a knee while he spoke to all of them at once. Now he could do that on his smartphone, except with the phone, there was no limit to how many people he could speak to.

To be efficient, of course, he used texting shorthand: *u* for *you*, *r* for *are*, *c* for *see*. When he reached the end of his allotted characters midword, he would start the next text just where he'd left off.

Jeremy's text messages spoke of everyday life, of challenges that he knew his readers faced. Never did he talk about himself. Never did he dwell on his personal limitations. And when he asked for prayer, it tended to be for one of Jacob's needs or those of someone else. Often though, he just sent out simple words of encouragement.

A typical text:

2 Cor. 4. "We are hard pressed on every side, but not crushed; perplexed, but not in despair; persecuted, but not abandoned; struck down, but not destroyed." My Daddy's got my back. Do you let him have yours? Not just on Sunday, during hard times, or daily, but moment by moment? Love u, Jeremy.

Another:

A Christian is defined as a follower of Jesus Christ. My wife always says, "If you want God to laugh, tell him 'your' plans." I say, "Jesus, take the wheel, so we can really enjoy the ride." Is he laughing at you or driving for you? Love ya, Jeremy.

There was no regular schedule for these texts. Quite often, God would give him a word during the night, and he would send it out the next day.

At first Jeremy sent texts to just a small circle of friends.

But soon people were calling and saying, "Why don't I get these texts I'm hearing about?" Name after name was added to the list. People everywhere were asking for the Scripture, the prayers, the wise little observations that came from the humble spirit and the trembling but still cooperative thumb of Jeremy Williams— the power of Christ proven out in earthly weaknesses.

Passages of this book were detailed through long series of short text messages. Jeremy would be exhausted after such a message. But he thanked God for that thumb and the thoughts and encouragement that could flow through it to the world, and his smile would be wider than ever as he thought about that.

That smile, it seemed, was one physical part of Jeremy that was stronger than ever.

What About You?

This last epic chapter of Jeremy Williams's life began with a hurt thumb—nothing more than a hand injured in a football practice. Then he watched in helplessness as he lost his grip first in that hand and eventually in the other.

In time, however, he came to understand that life is all about a grip that has nothing to do with bones and ligaments. It's the grip that Christ has on our lives. Then it's the grip we must have upon him.

Paul perfectly captured that double grip as he wrote to his friends in Philippi about his goal to know Christ fully and to experience his resurrection power: "Not that I have already obtained all this, or have already arrived at my goal, but I press on to take hold of that for which Christ Jesus took hold of me" (Phil. 3:12).

Jeremy knew that the meaning of life is summarized in those thirteen words: *to take hold of that for which Christ Jesus took hold of me.* It was all about getting a tenacious grip because of the tenacious grip Christ had upon him.

Jesus said about us, "I give them eternal life, and they shall never perish; no one will snatch them out of my hand" (John 10:28).

That's holding fast. That's *tenacious.*

As Jeremy sent his text messages, this was his challenge to all who listened, his challenge to all who would read this book:

- *What about you?* (All of his texts ended with some variation on those three words, challenging, coaching the readers to examine themselves in a fresh and honest way.)
- *How about it?* Have you allowed Jesus Christ to take hold of your life? If so, no one will snatch you away. But you, too, need to take hold of *him*—with a tenacious grip.

Jeremy would ask, "What is Jesus saying to you right now? What has been stirring in your spirit as you read these texts, as you turned the pages of this book? He is relentlessly pursuing you—are you relentlessly pursuing him?"

Life is wonderful, life is full, and life is very short. We can't measure the far end of it. All we can do is make this end of it count for him. So the question becomes:

- What are you doing for him today? How are you coming to know him more deeply, more joyfully, than you knew him yesterday?
- How are you glorifying him through your relationships—even in their points of weakness?

- How are you glorifying him through the work of your hands, even if your hands aren't doing all the work that they once could?
- How are you glorifying him through your time? Your possessions? Through this very moment?

Jeremy would say that whether you are young and healthy or whether you, like him, have little more than a shaky thumb, Jesus has you in his powerful grip, a grip nothing can weaken, no one can threaten, no circumstance can overcome. Once you know how infinitely, eternally tenacious his grip is, then you, through faith, can have the same tenacious grip on him.

That's when the adventures began for Jeremy.

And he testifies that it's also when the adventures can begin for you.

ACKNOWLEDGMENTS

OUR LORD AND SAVIOR JESUS CHRIST, HOW COULD WE ever thank you enough for the sacrifice of your life? We are so deeply humbled by the love, grace, and faithfulness that you show us moment by moment as we trust your plan for our lives. We thank you for the awesome privilege of telling your story for the Williams family. We lay this book at the foot of the cross as a gift to you, our precious Savior. We pray, Lord, that you will use the words of this book to broaden and enhance your kingdom. We love you, Lord, and thank you for being so good to us. We are nothing without you.

Josie, our darling firstborn, our favorite daughter. You are so beautiful. God's goodness and passion shine from you. You are our Crusader and we wait with breathless expectation to see the blessings that God has just for you.

Jacob, our handsome fella, our favorite son. You are our "clutch" player. You rise to the challenge. Watching your steadfast determination always inspires us. God has big plans and you are the man for the job.

We love y'all with all our hearts. God has truly blessed us with the very best children ever. And we are so thankful to Him for choosing us to be your parents—it is our pleasure indeed.

Mom, Dad, Mama G, Kim, and the rest of the family, how

could we ever survive this journey without you? Your constant love, encouragement, and assistance are so deeply appreciated. We love you all the way to the moon and back.

Andy and Jason, we thank you for encouraging us to share the story that God has laid before us. Whoever would have known . . . ?

Rob, we cannot even imagine the challenges that come with writing a story from many text messages and the ramblings of a tired lady. We are so very thankful to you for your patience as you pursued even the smallest details. You have a God-given talent, our friend, and you use it for His glory! We thank God for picking you! And we thank you for pursuing!

Andy, Mike, Jason, and Pete, thank you for providing us the opportunity to begin this book. To each one of you, thank you for using your God-given gifts to help God's story for the Williams family be told. You all are precious to us and we are so thankful for you.

Greg, thank you for always keeping us moving forward in the work. With a life like ours we need that person who keeps us streamlined. Thank you.

Jonathan, thank you for taking the time to clarify for us those things that we wanted to share about Christ. Your help was invaluable and we are so appreciative of you. You have a special gift and we thank you for continuing to deepen our knowledge of Christ through His blessing of open eyes.

Doug and Dianna, thank you for reviewing the delicate pages of *Tenacious* for us. Your wisdom and thoughts proved invaluable.

Thomas Nelson, thank you for being a company that wants to publish a book that will bring God glory. For standing firm in your mission to the world—to honor God. Thank you for choosing *Tenacious*. May the lives of many be changed for the Kingdom because of you.

Kristen, thank you for the patience that you showed us as we went back and forth about the subtitle. You never rushed us as we waited on God and we thank you.

Sweet, precious, Janene. You are such a blessing to us. You displayed God's grace over and over to us and we are so thankful for your kindness and your encouragement. You are a fine lady of God!

Anne, thank you for your attention to detail. You truly challenged us in the smallest of details. Thank you for doing such a beautiful job.

To all the rest of the crew at Thomas Nelson, thank you. Although we do not know all those involved with the work that is *Tenacious*, we thank you for using your specific talents for God's kingdom.

To the ladies of play group, you have sustained us in all things. Thank you for the love, support, and laughs. As Jennifer V. says, "Together we make the perfect lady!"

To our communities, we thank you for the love and support that you constantly shower upon us. We have always felt blessed to live where we live!

To all our friends in Meriwether County, there are not many school systems that would have allowed Jeremy to continue to "do what we do." We thank you for all the support you have always shown our family. You are precious to us!

To our many friends, our church Edgewood Baptist, our prayer warriors, thank you. When you agreed to our friendships, you probably never realized how high maintenance we would be. But you have stayed the course and our family would not be who we are without you.

To all those that had anything to do with the building of our home or the making of our show, we humbly thank you for providing a home that is a castle made perfect for the Williams family. We are so thankful for you and pray God's special blessings upon you.

And lastly, to our readers, Jeremy and I would like to say thank you for taking the time to read this book. Time is precious. You don't live our circumstances without figuring that out quickly. So thank you for taking time out of your daily life to read the story that God has given our family to walk out for His Glory. You know, we all have a choice, every day, every hour, every minute—do we lay down our story (our plans, our dreams, etc.) and live out the story that God ordained for our lives, or do we not? What would happen if we, as an individual, as a church, as a world gave our all to Christ? What would happen if we made the decision to be—Tenacious.

NOTES

Chapter 2: Columbus Days

1. From the screenplay by Collin Welland, quoted in "Memorable Quotes for *Chariots of Fire*," International Movie Data Base, http://www.imdb.com/title/tt0082158/quotes.

Chapter 4: Finding Focus

1. Richard Hyatt, "Greenville rallies around Jeremy Williams," *Columbus Ledger-Enquirer,* November 26, 2009, http://www .ledger-enquirer.com/2009/11/26/922362/greenville-rallies-around-jeremy.html.
2. Spencer Hall, "An Interview with Hal Mumme, College Football's All-Time David," SB Nation, June 26, 2012, http:// www.sbnation.com/ncaa-football/2012/6/26/3118498/hal-mumme-interview, accessed March 28, 2013.

Chapter 6: High-Impact Faith

1. "Chuck Stobart Show," Memphis-area TV, 1991; recently shown on YouTube, not presently available (updated March 28, 2013).
2. Interview, recalled/reported by Jeremy and Jennifer Williams.

Chapter 14: Gut Check

1. Gary D. Chapman, *The 5 Love Languages: The Secret to Love That Lasts,* new ed. (Chicago: Northfield, 2009).

NOTES

CHAPTER 15: WE DO WHAT WE DO
1. Denise Glenn, *Restore My Heart: God's Passionate Love for His Bridge* (Houston: Kardo International Ministries, 2002). For more about Denise Glenn's ministry, consult her website at http://www.kardo.org/contact.

CHAPTER 16: WELCOME TO THE FRONT LINE
1. Louie Giglio, *Hope: When Life Hurts Most* (Roswell, GA: Six Step Records, 2009), DVD.
2. Ted Dekker, *Adam* (Nashville: Thomas Nelson, 2008).

ABOUT THE AUTHORS

Jeremy Williams, now retired, played college football at the University of Memphis and coached at three high schools in Georgia, including nine years as head coach at Greenville High School, where he was named National High School Coach of the Year in 2010.

Jennifer Williams, Jeremy's wife, cares for her husband and two children, the younger of whom has spina bifida. She is an Assistive Technology Specialist for special needs children and a horse enthusiast.